# POLITICAL THOUGHTS AND ORGANISATION IN CENTRAL INDIA
## (The Early Medieval Period)

# POLITICAL THOUGHTS AND ORGANISATION IN CENTRAL INDIA
## (The Early Medieval Period)

GARIMA UPADHYAY

SHARADA

SHARADA PUBLISHING HOUSE
DELHI

*First Published 2010*


ISBN: 978-81-88934-64-5



*Published by*
Anjana Bansal
**SHARADA PUBLISHING HOUSE**
111, Vidya Vihar Apartment
Sector-9, Rohini, Delhi- 110085
Ph.: +91-11-3292 1560, 2755 2102
E-mail: books@sharadabooks.com,
bansal_sph@rediffmail.com
Website : www.sharadabooks.com

*Printed at*
Salasar Imaging Systems
Delhi

# CONTENTS

# PREFACE

Central India comprising of Madhya Pradesh and Chhattisgarh was a playground of Political forces during the early medieval period on account of the rule of powerful dynasties like the Pratihāras, the Rāṣṭrakūṭas, the Paramāras, the Kalachuris, the Candellas, the Kacchapaghāṭas, the Yajvapālas, the Nāgas of Bastar etc. Each of these dynasties played a dominant role in shaping the political history not only the region over which they ruled, but northern, eastern, western and southern India where they often carried on raids and established their supremacy. Their conquests were carried as far as Bengal and Orissa in the east, Gujarat in the west, Kashmir in the north and Karnataka in the south. Also their cultural achievements in the field of Art, Literature, Religion and Society were immense. All these were possible only on account of sound policies the rulers followed and achieved them through the thoughts of ancient Indian political thinkers. What was the nature of the political thought and organization of the ruling dynasties of Central India during the post - Harṣa period, till the rise of the Muslim rule in this part of the country is the subject matter of research in this book. No work on the lines suggested hereinunder has been attempted till date.

The primary source of the present study is inscriptions of the Rāṣṭrakūṭas, the Kalachuris, the Paramāras, the Candellas, the Pratihāras, the Kacchapaghāṭas, the Nāgas and the Yajvapālas who were ruling over different parts of the region. These sources of information have further been supplemented by the contemporary literary works of the court-poets of the rulers concerned, in addition to other contemporary literary sources. Various *Smṛtis, Nīti* works and Digests have been suitably employed to supplement the findings. Numismatic sources too have been harnessed to arrive at conclusions. Interpretations provided in Modern works have been utilized wherever necessary.

Throughout the course of this study, the author has tried to remain objective and has not allowed any preconceived notions to supervise her analysis. If she has differed at several places from the authorities, it is only because her findings have led her to such conclusions. For this she extends her apologies to them with due regards.

The author expresses her deep gratitude to Dr. R.K. Sharma, Retd. Professor of Ancient Indian History, Culture and Archaeology, Rani Durgavati Vishwavidyalaya, Jabalpur, who infused in her the desire to conduct research on this neglected aspects of administrative history of early medieval India. The author will fail in her duty if she does not express her gratefulness to her husband, Shri M.M. Upadhyay, IAS, for his sustained interest in her work. But for his constant support and encouragement, the present work would not have seen the light of the day.

**Garima Upadhyay**

## CHAPTER I

# AN OUTLINE HISTORY OF INDIA

Central India comprising of modern Madhya Pradesh and Chhattisgarh was a playground of political forces during the early medieval period (*c.* 7th century A.D. to 13th century A.D.) on account of the rule of such powerful dynasties like the Pratihāras, the Rāṣṭrakūṭas, the Paramāras, the Kalachuris, the Candellas, the Kacchapaghāṭas, the Yajvapālas, the Nāgas etc. in addition to minor dynasties. Each of these dynasties played a dominant role in shaping the political history not only of the region on which they ruled, but northern, eastern, western and southern India where they they often carried on raids and established their supremacy. Their conquests were carried out as far as Bengal and Orissa in the east, Gujarat in the west, Kashmir in the north and Karnataka in the south. An outline history of the dynasties concerned and their role in Central India may be presented as follows:

### The Rāṣṭrakūṭas

One of the earlier branches of the Rāṣṭrakūṭas was ruling in the Betul-Amravati region during 7th-8th century

A.D. Two copper-plates of Nannarāja Yuddhāsura of this dynasty, dated in Śaka Era 553 and 631 have been respectively found at Tiwarkhed and Multai, both in the Betul district.[1] Possibly towards the end of 8th century A.D. this branch was subdued by the main branch of the Rāṣṭrakūṭas ruling in the Deccan.

The most powerful rulers of the Rāṣṭrakūṭa dynasty of Manyakheta were Dantidurga, Kṛṣṇa I, Govinda II, Dhruva and Govinda III. The last named ruler actively participated in the tripartite struggle for supremacy over Kannauja that took place among the Rāṣṭrakūṭas, the Gurjara Pratihāras and the Pālas. It was through Madhya Pradesh that the Rāṣṭrakūṭa armies marched to Northern India. The Indragarh (Mandsaur distt.) stone inscription makes reference of him as well as of Indra III.[2] His successors continued the policy of the invasion of Northern India. That Kṛṣṇa III made conquest of Bundeḷkhand region of M.P. is evident from the stone inscription of his reign found at Jura, near Maihar in the Satna district.[3] Two more inscriptions from Nīlakaṇṭhī in the Chhindwara district also refer to the reign of Kṛṣṇa III.[4] Inscriptions of some of the feudatories of the Rāṣṭrakūṭas have also been found from M.P. These are: The Bahuriband Jaina image inscription of Mahāsāmantādhipati Golhaṇadeva[5], the Piparia (Damoh) stone pillar inscription of Mahāmaṇḍalika Rāṇaka Jayatsiṁha[6] Pathari (Vidisha) stone inscription of Rāṣṭrakūṭa Parabala[7] and the Jethwai (Nimar) copper plate inscription of a Rāṣṭrakūṭa queen dated in Śaka Era 708.[8] These inscriptions indicate that the Rāṣṭrakūṭas played an important part in the political history of Central India during ancient period.[9]

**The Gurjara Pratihāras of Ujjain and Kannauja**

In the first quarter of 8th century A.D. a branch of the Gurjara Pratihāras was established at Ujjain.[10] Nāgabhaṭa II, Vatsarāja and Nāgabhaṭa II, the rulers of this branch of the Gurjara Pratihāras clashed with and were defeated by the contemporary Rāṣṭrakūṭa rulers who invaded Northern India from time to time. During the reign of Nāgabhaṭa II, capital of the dynasty was shifted from Ujjain to Kannauja.

From an inscription found at Gwalior[11] it is known that the area was included in the Gurjara Pratihāra Empire during the reign of Rāmabhadra, the successor of Nāgabhaṭa II. Three inscriptions of Mihira Bhoja, the successor of Rāmabhadra, found at Gwalior[12] confirm that the concerned area formed a part of his territory. To keep his sway over Ujjain, Mihira Bhoja had to fight with Rāṣṭrakūṭa Amoghavarṣa and Kṛṣṇa II. The territory around Guna continued to be a part of the Gurjara Pratihāra empire is indicated by an inscription of Vināyakapāladeva found at Rakhetara (Guna).[13]

Even after the fall of the imperial branch of the Gurjara Pratihāras of Kannauja, three minor Pratihāra branches continued to rule in the districts of Guna, Shivpuri, Jabalpur and Damoh. This is indicated by inscriptions of the respective dynasties found at Chanderi and Kadwaha,[14] Kuraitha[15] and in Jabalpur-Damoh region.[16]

**The Candellas**

The Candellas succeeded the Gurjara-Pratihāras in the Bundelkhand region of M.P. Their territory comprised not only of Bundelkhand but part of Uttar

Pradesh also where large number of their inscriptions have been found. They ruled between the first quarter of 9th century A.D. to the end of the 13th century A.D.[17]

The two earliest known Candella inscriptions are those of Dhaṅga (950-1000 A.D.) found at Khajuraho. The inscriptions dated in V.S. 1011 and 1059[18] along with evidence provided by other inscriptions show that Dhaṅga was the first ruler of this dynasty who threw off allegiance of the Pratihāras and declared himself independent. The next known inscription is the copper plate grant of Vidyādhara dated in V.E. 1060 (1004 A.D.) found from Kundeshwar.[19] Copper-plate charter of Devavarman dated in V.S. 1108 found from Charkhari[20] is the next dated record. His period was full of troubles as the Kalachuris of Tripuri had defeated him. An inscription dated in V.S. 1173 found from Khajuraho belonging to the reign Sallakṣaṇavarman is the next dated Candella inscription.[21] The reign of Madanavarman was glorious in the history of the Candellas. Of the thirteen inscriptions of his reign six have been found from Ajaigarh[22], Chhatarpur[23], Khajuraho[24] and Papaura[25] and the rest from U.P. A hoard of 48 silver coins of his reign has been located at Rewa.[26] The prestige of the empire was well-preserved by his successor Paramardideva. Twelve inscriptions of his reign have till now been found. Of these seven have been located in M.P., at Ajaigarh[27], Ahar,[28] Charkhari[29], Madanpur[30], Semra[31] and Kundeshwar[32]; the rest from U.P.

The son and successor of Paramardi was Trailokyavarman. Eight inscriptions of his reign have been found till now. Of these, seven have been located in M.P. at Rewa,[33] Ajaigarh,[34] Sagar,[35] Garra,[36] and

Ramban.[37] A copper coin issued by him has also been found at Hoshangabad[38] and a gold coin from Ajaigarh.[39]

The next ruler was his son Vīravarman, eight out of ten of whose inscriptions have been located in M.P. at Ajaigarh[40], Gurha[41], Charkhari[42] and Dahi.[43] Gold drammas issued by him have been fund at Khajuraho and Tripuri.[44]

Bhojavarman succeeded Vīravarman. Three inscriptions of his times have been found at Ajaigarh[45] and Ishvarmau.[46] These do not supply details about the events of his reign.

Hammīravarman succeeded Bhojavarman. Three known inscriptions of his reign are from Ajaigarh[47], Charkhari[48] and Bamhani.[49] The inscriptions prove his control even on Ḍāhala maṇḍala in addition to his own territories. An inscription of his successor Vīravarman II has been found at Ladvari. The inscription is damaged.[50] However, by the first decade of the 14th century A.D., the power of the imperial dynasty of the Candellas of Jejākabhukti fell.

**The Paramāras**

The Paramāras of Malwa were contemporaries of the Candellas. The founder of the dynasty was Upendra and he was successively followed by Vairisiṁha, Siyaka I, Vākpati I, Vairisiṁha II, Siyaka II and Muñja.[51] Six inscriptions of the reign of Muñja have been found from Ujjain[52], Gaonri[53] and Dharampur.[54] Muñja was succeeded by Sindhurāja and Bhoja I. Twelve inscriptions of the latter's reign dated between V.S. 1074 and 1091 located at Ujjain,[55] Depalpur,[56] Dhar[57], Betma[58], Bhojpur,[59] and Mahandi[60] throw important light on the political and cultural achievements of this legendary figure of Indian History.

Bhoja was succeeded by Jayasiṁha, one of whose copper plate inscriptions dated in V.S. 1112 has been located at Mandhata.[61] The inscription records some donations made by the ruler.

The successor of Jayasiṁha was Udayāditya, eight inscriptions of whose reign have been found at Ujjain,[62] Udaipur,[63] Un,[64] Dhar[65] and Bhopal.[66] He was responsible for construction of the Nīlakaṇṭheśvara temple at Udaipur. His gold coins have been located at Indore.[67]

Lakṣmaṇadeva succeeded Udayāditya. Soon he abdicated his throne in favour of his brother Naravarman. The reign of Naravarman was full of troubles and this is evidenced by inscriptions of his period found at Ujjain[68], Udaipur,[69] Dhar,[70] Bhojpur,[71] Dewas[72] and Indore.[73] Gold and copper coins issued by him have been located at Indore[74].

Yaśovarman succeeded Naravarman. His copper plate grant dated in V.E. 1192 has been found at Ujjain.[75] He had to face great calamities on account of invasion of Cāḷukya Jayasiṁha Siddharāja of Gujarat who not only conquered Malwa but imprisoned Yaśovarman. Cāḷukya occupation of Malwa till V.S.1195 is evidenced by Siddharāja's inscription found at Ujjain.[76]

Jayavarman, son of Yaśovarman, re-conquered Malwa during the last days of Siddharāja but this proved to be a temporary phase as Malwa continued to be occupied by the Cāḷukyas till the seventh decade of 12th century A.D. as is evidenced by the inscriptions of Kumārapāla dated in V.S. 1220 and 1222[77] and the inscription of Ajayapāla dated in V.S. 1229,[78] found at Udaipur. During the period of eclipse the Paramāras ruled as feudatories of the Cāḷukyas and this is evidenced by their inscriptions found at Ujjain[79], Pipliyanagar[80], Bhopal[81] and Hoshangabad.[82]

Malwa was re-occupied by the Paramāras during the reign of Vindhyavarman, son of Jayavarman but the period of his reign was full of troubles. He was succeeded by Subhaṭavarman and Arjunavarman. One stone inscription at Dhar,[83] one copper-plate grant at Pipliyanagar[84] and two copper plate grants at Bhopal[85] all belonging to the reign of Arjunavarman have till now been located.

Devapāla succeeded Arjunavarman. His inscriptions found from Ujjain,[86] Udaipur,[87] Okhla,[88] Karnavad[89], Mandhata[90] and Harauda[91] indicate that these regions were still within his territorial jurisdiction.

The two successors of Arjunavarman were Jaitugideva and Jayavarman II. Four inscriptions of the reign of the latter have been found at Godarpura[92], Modi[93], Rahatgarh[94] and Bamai[95].

Jayasiṁha II succeeded Jayavarman II. Four inscriptions of his times found at Udaipur[96], Walipur[97] and Pathari[98] throw light on the events of his reign.

The last three rulers of this dynasty were respectively Arjunavarman II, Bhoja II and Mahālakadeva. By the first decade of the fourteenth century A.D. Malwa was conquered by the Muslims.

## The Kalachuris

### *(a) The Kalachuris of Māhiṣmatī*

The ancient capital of the Kalachuris was at Māhiṣmatī where they rose to power in the 6th century A.D.[99] Three rulers of this dynasty were Kṛṣṇarāja, Śaṅkaragaṇa and

Buddharāja whose copper-plate inscriptions have been found at Abhona, Saṅkhera, Vadner and Sarsavni in Maharashtra and Gujarat. Coins of Kṛṣṇarāja have been found at Tewar, Besnagar and Pattan.[100] Their power was eclipsed by the rise of the Cāḷukyas of the Deccan.

***(b) The Kalachuris of Tripuri***

This branch of the Kalachuri dynasty was founded by Vāmarāja. Three generations after him was ruling Śaṅkaragaṇa I, two inscriptions whose reign have been found at Chhoti Deori and Sagar.[101] On the basis of these two inscriptions the period of his rule has been placed in the middle of 8th century A.D.

The next known Kalachuri ruler war Lakṣmaṇarāja whose inscription dated in K.E. 593 has been found at Karitalai.[102] He was succeeded respectively by Kokalla I, Śaṅkaragaṇa II, Bālaharṣa and Yuvarājadeva I. Though no inscriptions of their reign have been found, on the basis of information supplied by the inscriptions of their successors it has been possible to know that the empire of the Kalachuris had been extended far and wide during their regime. Lakṣmaṇarāja II succeeded Yuvarājadeva I and like his father, he was a powerful ruler. An inscription of his reign found at Karitalai,[103] along with other evidences indicate that he conquered many countries. He was succeeded by Śaṅkaragaṇa III and latter by Yuvarāja II. The Bilahari stone inscription of his reiġn[104] indicates that Tripuri had to see bad days when he was ruling. The Gurgi stone inscription[105] of his successor Kokalladeva II hints that renewed efforts were made to retrieve the fortunes of the empire. In 1015 A.D. Gāṅgeyadeva succeeded the Kalachuri throne and two inscriptions of his reign found at Makundpur[106] and Piawan[107] and evidences provided by the inscriptions of his successors show that he proved to be the most powerful ruler of the Kalachuri dynasty known till then. Gold and Silver coins issued by him have been found at Isurpur[108], Tewar[109], Baretha[110], Barela[111], Mandu[112], Sagar[113], Sonsari[114], Tripuri[115], Jargawan[116] and Dugaria.[117]

Karṇa, the son and successor of Gāṅgeyadeva proved more competent than his father. For his political achievement he is known as Hindu Napolean. Of the nine inscriptions of his times four have been located in M.P. at Rewa,[118] Simra and Simaria.[119]

Karṇa abdicated his throne in favour of his son Yaśaḥkarṇa in 1073 A.D. Three inscriptions of his reign found at Khairha[120], Jabalpur[121] and Barhi[122] supported by other evidences indicate that he failed to keep intact the empire that he inherited.

Two inscriptions of the reign of his successor Gayākarṇa are found at Tewar and Bahuriband,[123] three inscriptions of the reign of the next ruler Narasiṁha found at Alhaghat, Bheraghat and Lal Pahar[124] and five inscriptions of the latter's successor Jayasiṁha located at Karanbel, Tewar, Jabalpur and Rewa[125] prove that the fortunes of the Kalachuri empire could not be revived in spite of the best efforts of the rulers concerned. The situation grew worse during the regime of Vijayasiṁha, eight inscriptions of whose times have till now been found at Karanbel, Tewar, Bheraghat, Kumbhi, Rewa, Umaria and Jhulpur.[126] He was succeeded by Pratāpamalla one of whose inscriptions has been located at Dhureti.[127] Trailokyamalla is the last known ruler of the Kalachuris of Tripuri. When and how his reign came to an end is not known in the existing state of knowledge.

*(c) The Kalachuris of Ratanpur*

A new branch of the *Kalachuri dynasty* ruling from Ratanpur in the Bilaspur district of M.P. was founded by Kaliṅgarāja around 1000 A.D. He was successively followed by Kamalarāja, Ratnarāja and Pṛthvīdeva I. Three inscriptions of Pṛthvīdeva I found at Amoda[128], Lapha and Raipur indicate that he was still ruling as a feudatory of the Kalachuris of Tripuri. His successor was Jājalladeva I, two inscriptions of whose reign have been located at Pali and Ratanpur.[129] The next ruler was Ratnadeva II, four inscriptions of whose rule found at Akaltara, Pargaon, Sheorinarayan and Sarkho[130] provide details about the period of his rule. Pṛthvīdeva II was his successor and fifteen inscriptions issued during his regime throw important light on the political and cultural history of the period.[131] The Amoda, Malhar and Sheori Narayan inscriptions[132] of the reign of the next ruler Jājalladeva show that his period of rule was short and full of troubles. He was succeeded by Ratnadeva II, whose two inscriptions have been located at Kharod and Pasid.[133] The latter was succeeded by Pratāpamalla, two Copperplate inscriptions and coins of whose regime have been found.[134] These, however, do not help us to reconstruct the history of the period. Political history of this branch of the Kalachuris is not clear after the rule of Pratāpamalla.

A hoard of 3,900 coins of the different rulers of the Kalachuris of Ratanpur has been located at Dhanpur.[135] Coins of rulers of this dynasty have also been and at

Dalalseoni, Balpur, Bhagaund, Sarangarh and Sonsari.[136] A hoard of 139 coins issued by Jājalladeva and Ratnadeva have been found at Kera, distt. Bilaspur.[137] The problem of attribution of these coins is still a matter of keen controversy among scholars.

### *(d) The Kalachuris of Raipur*

It was around the end of 14th century A.D. that the Ratanpur branch of the Kalachuri dynasty was divided into two. The main branch ruled at Ratanpur and a subordinate branch was founded at Raipur. The relations of these two branches have been made clear by inscriptions of Vāhara found at Kosgain and Ratanpur[138] and the two inscriptions of Brahmadeva located at Raipur and Khalari.[139] The dynasty was ruling till 18th century A.D. when it was supplanted by the Marathas.

## The Trikaliṅgādhipati Somavaṁśīs

During 10th century A.D. a major part of South Kosala was ruled by the Trikaliṅgādhipati Somavaṁśī rulers of Orissa. However, none of their inscriptions has been located within the territorial jurisdiction of M.P.

## The Chindaka Nāgas of Cakrakoṭa (Bastar)

It was in the 11th century A.D. that a Nāga dynasty known as the Chindaka Nāgas established their rule over, Cakrokoṭa, now known as Bastar. The Errakota inscription[140] provides details about Nripatibhūṣaṇa, the first ruler of this dynasty. Light on the activities of the next ruler Dhārāvarṣa Jagadekabhūṣaṇa is thrown by his Barsur and Bhairamgarh inscriptions.[141] He was succeeded by Madhurāntakadeva, a copper plate inscription of whose regime has been located at Rajpur.[142] The next ruler was Someśvara, political events of whose regime are known by inscriptions found at Kuruspal and Gadia.[143] An inscription issued by his wife Gaṅgamahādevī was found at Barsur[144] and another issued by his mother Guṇḍamahādevī located at Nārāyanpāla.[145] A hoard of 600 coins of Someśvara was located at Sonsari.[146] An inscription found at Barsur[147] refers to a ruler, Kannaradeva of this dynasty. The Jatanpal[148] and Dantewara[149] stone inscriptions refer to Jagadekabhūṣaṇa Mahārāja Narasiṁhadeva of this lineage. An inscription found at Sunarpāla[150] mentions the name of Jayasiṁhadeva and another located at Temra[151] refers to Hariścandra of this dynasty but the details about the last two rulers are not available.

**The Nāgas of Kawardha**

The Nāgas of Kawardha established their power in 9th century A.D. and they continued their rule till the middle of 14th century A.D. as feudatories of the Kalachuris of Ratanpur. Details about this dynasty have been supplied by nine inscriptions found at Kawardha, Chaura, Chhapri, Pujaripali, Boria and Sahaspur.[152]

**The Somavaṁśīs of Kanker**

An inscription found at Kanker[153] proves the existence of a Somavaṁśī dynasty ruling there who were subordinates of the Kalachuris of Ratanpur. Six more inscriptions of this dynasty have been located at Gurur, Tahankapar, Deokut and Sihawa.[154]

**The Yādavas of Deogiri**

The Yādavas of Deogiri ruling in 11th-12th century A.D. had extended their sway over parts of M.P. The extensions made by Yādava Siṁhaṇa is indicated by his inscription found at Balaghat[155] and that of Rāmacandra by the Lanji pillar inscription.[156] Their coins have been located at Kotha, Dewas and Parsadih.[157]

**The Cāḷukyas of Anahilapataka**

The Cāḷukyas of Anahilapataka too had incursions in M.P. in course of their extension activities. Five inscriptions of their rulers found at Ujjain, Udaipur and Bilpak[158] throw light on their political activities in this part of the country.

**The Guhilas of Mandsaur**

Six Inscriptions found at Jiran[159] in Mandsaur district of M.P. prove existence of the dynasty of the Guhilas ruling in 10th century A.D. at Mandsaur. Details about the achievements of the rulers of this dynasty are supplied by these inscriptions.

**The Kacchapaghāṭas**

The Kacchapaghāṭas rose into prominence at Gwalior and the neighbouring region between 10th-12th century A.D. Three of their branches were ruling at Gwalior, Dubkund and Narwar. Light on the political history of the Kacchapaghāṭas of Gwalior is thrown by inscriptions of this dynasty found at Ingnod, Kulwar. Gwalior, Tilori and Naresar.[160] An inscription found at Dubkund[161] provides details about the Dubkund branch of this dynasty. Another copper-plate inscription located at

Narwar[162] supplies details of the political events of the rulers of the Narwar branch of the Kacchapaghāṭas.

### The Yajvapālas of Narwar

The dynasty of the Yajvapālas ruling at Narwar came into prominence in the later half of 13th century A.D. The dynasty was founded by Chāhaḍa whose inscriptions have been found at Udaipur[163] and Bhaktar.[164] He also issued coins which are dated between 1237 and 1254 A.D.[165] The next ruler was Āsalladeva, events of whose reign have been provided by inscriptions found at Narwar, Baraudi, Bhimpur and Budhi Rai.[166] His coins datable between 1254 and 1279 A.D. have also been found.[167] Gopāladeva succeeded him and thirteen inscriptions of his reign have been found at Narwar, Bangla, Balarpur, Pachrai and Barhotar.[168] The last ruler of this dynasty was Gaṇapati and eleven inscriptions of the period of his rule found at Tilori, Narwar, Paharo, Balarpur, Bhesarwas, Surwaya and Mukhwasa[169] supply details about his achievements. Possibly he was defeated by Alauddin Khalji.

## REFERENCES

1. Sharma, R.K., *Madhya Pradesh ke Purātattva kā Sandarbha Granth,* nos. 726, 731.
2. *Ibid.*, 722-b.
3. *Ibid.*, 724.
4. *Ibid.*, 727-a, b.
5. *Ibid.*, 730.
6. *Ibid.*, 729.
7. *Ibid.*, 728.

8. *Ibid.*, 725.
9. For Detailed history of the Rāṣṭrakūṭas, see Altekar, A.S.: *Rāṣṭrakūṭas and their Times*, Poona, 1934.
10. For a detailed history of the Gurjara Pratihāras, See Puri, B.N. : *The History of the Gurjara Pratihāras*, Bombay, 1957.
11. *Ibid.*, 735-c.
12. *Ibid.*, 735-a, a 743.
13. *Ibid.*, 740.
14. *Ibid.*, 733 a, b, c, 736-a, b; *IAR*, 1970-71, p. 48.
15. *Ibid.*, 734 a, b.
16. *Ibid.*, 732, 737, 739, 741, 742, 744.
17. For a detailed of history of the Candellas, see Dikshit, R.K. : *The Candellas of Jejakabhukti*, Delhi, 1977.
18. *Ibid.*, 749.
19. *IAR* 1971-72, p. 55.
20. *MPSG* 752-9.
21. *Ibid.*, 749-e.
22. *Ibid.*, 745-a.
23. *Ibid.*, 753.
24. *Ibid.*, 749 f-h.
25. *Ibid.*, 757.
26. *Ibid.*, 2391.
27. *Ibid.*, 745-b-c.
28. *Ibid.*, 746-b; *IAR*, 1971-72, p. 55.
29. *Ibid.*, 752-b.
30. *Ibid.*, 759.
31. *Ibid.*, 763.
32. *IAR*, 1971-72, p. 55.
33. *Ibid.*, 761-a-c.
34. *Ibid.*, 745-d.
35. *Ibid.*, 762.
36. *Ibid.*, 750.
37. *Ibid.*, 760.

38. *Ibid.*, 2391/1.
39. *JNSI,* XXXIV, pt. II, pp. 262-63.
40. *MPSG,* 745, e, f, g, h, i.
41. *Ibid.*, 751.
42. *Ibid.*, 752-e.
43. *Ibid.*, 755.
44. *Ibid.*, 2390, 2392.
45. *Ibid.*, 745 j, k, l.
46. *Ibid.*, 747.
47. *Ibid.*, 745-n.
48. *Ibid.*, 752-d.
49. *Ibid.*, 758.
50. *IAR* 1971-72, pp. 55-56.
51. For detailed History of the Paramāras, See Bhatia, P. : *The Paramāras,* Delhi.
52. *MPSG,* 766-a, b, c.
53. *Ibid.*, 772.
54. *Ibid.*, 775.
55. *Ibid.*, 766 m (1); 766-d; *IAR,* 1980-81, p. 81.
56. *Ibid.*, 774.
57. *Ibid.*, 776-a, 776-c.
58. *Ibid.*, 780.
59. *Ibid.*, 781-a.
60. *Ibid.*, 783.
61. *Ibid.*, 784-a.
62. *Ibid.*, 766-j.
63. *Ibid.*, 767-a, b, j; *IAR,* 1974-75, p. 55.
64. *Ibid.*, 769.
65. *Ibid.*, 776-e.
66. *Ibid.*, 782-a, b.
67. *Ibid.*, 2393.b.
68. *Ibid.*, 766-i, m-5; *IAR,* 1969-70, p.47.
69. *Ibid.*, 767-j.
70. *Ibid.*, 776-d.

71. *Ibid.*, 781-b.
72. *IAR*, 1970-71, p. 48.
73. *IAR*, 1974-75, p. 55.
74. *MPSG*, 2393-a, c.
75. *Ibid.*, 766-c.
76. *Ibid.*, 878.
77. *Ibid.*, 879-a, b.
78. *Ibid.*, 879-c.
79. *Ibid.*, 766-ff.
80. *Ibid.*, 778-a.
81. *Ibid.*, 782 c, f.
82. *IAR*, 1971-72, p. 54, p. 6.
83. *MPSG*, 776-b.
84. *Ibid.*, 778-b.
85. *Ibid.*, 782-d, e.
86. *Ibid.*, 766-m-2.
87. *Ibid.*, 767-c, d.
88. *Ibid.*, 770.
89. *Ibid.*, 771-a, b.
90. *Ibid.*, 714-b.
91. *Ibid.*, 788.
92. *Ibid.*, 773.
93. *Ibid.*, 785.
94. *Ibid.*, 786.
95. *IAR*, 1978-79, p. 82.
96. *MPSG*, 767-e-f; *EI*, XXXVIII (1969-70), pt. 1, pp. 33-36.
97. *Ibid.*, 787.
98. *Ibid.*, 777; *EI*, XXXVII, (1969-70), pt. I, pp. 36-37.
99. For detailed History of the Kalachuris, See, Sharma, R.K.: *The Kalachuris and their Times*, Delhi.
100. *Ibid.*, nos. 2396, 2400, 2405.
101. *Ibid.*, 797,812.
102. *Ibid.*, 791-a.
103. *Ibid.*, 791-b.

104. *Ibid.*, 804-a.
105. *Ibid.*, 794.
106. *Ibid.*, 800
107. *Ibid.*, 807.
108. *Ibid.*, 2394.
109. *Ibid.*, 2396.
110. *Ibid.*, 2402.
111. *Ibid.*, 2403.
112. *Ibid.*, 2407.
113. *Ibid.*, 2410.
114. *Ibid.*, 2412.
115. *Ibid.*, 2413.
116. *JNSI*, XXXIX (1977). pt. 1 & 2, pp. 172 ff.
117. *IAR*, 1978-79, p. 90.
118. *MPSG*, 810-a, b.
119. *Ibid.*, 813; *IAR*, 1978-79, p. 82.
120. *Ibid.*, 793.
121. *Ibid.*, 798-a.
122. *IAR*, 1970-71, p. 48.
123. *MPSG*, 799-b; 802.
124. *Ibid.*, 789; 806-a; 811.
125. *Ibid.*, 790-a, 798 a, c; 799-c; 810 c.
126. *Ibid.*, 790-b, 792, 799-d, 806-b, 810-d, e; Sharma R.K., *The Kalachuris and their Times*, Delhi (1980), p. 35; *IAR*, 1976-77, p. 60; 77-78, p. 64.
127. Mirashi V.V., *CII*, IV, Ins. no. 72.
128. *MPSG*, 815-a, 831-a, 832.
129. *Ibid.*, 824, 829-a.
130. *Ibid.*, 814-a; 823-a; 833-a; 834.
131. *Ibid.*, 815, 816, 818, 821, 822, 823, 826, 828, 829, 830, 831; *IAR*, 1977-78, pp. 64-65.
132. *Ibid.*, 815-d; 837-a, 833-b .
133. *Ibid.*, Sharma, R.K.: *The Kalachuris and their Times*, pp. 309-10.

134. *MPSG*, no. 825; 826, 2404-b.
135. *Ibid.*, 2399.
136. *Ibid.*, 2397, 2404, 2406, 2411, 2412.
137. *IAR*,1978-79, p. 90.
138. *MPG*, 819-a, b, 829-e-f.
139. *Ibid.*, 837, 838.
140. *Ibid.*, 853.
141. *Ibid.*, 861-a; *IAR*, 1971-72, p. 53.
142. *Ibid.*, 863.
143. *Ibid.*, 854-a, b, d ; 855-a, b.
144. *Ibid.*, 861-b.
145. *Ibid.*, 859.
146. *Ibid.*, 2414.
147. *HL*, no. 292.
148. *MPSG*, no. 856.
149. *Ibid.*, 858-b.
150. *Ibid.*, 864.
151. *Ibid.*, 857.
152. *Ibid.*, nos. 865 to 870.
153. *Ibid.*, 871 a.
154. *Ibid.*, nos. 871-b to 875.
155. *Ibid.*, 876.
156. *Ibid.*, 877.
157. *Ibid.*, nos. 2415, 2416, 2417.
158. *Ibid.*, 878, 879-a, b, c, 879/1; *IAR*, 1969-70, p. 47.
159. *Ibid.*, 880 a-f.
160. *Ibid.*, 881, 882, 883 a-c, 884; *EI* XXXVIII (1969-70), pt. III, pp. 132-34.
161. *Ibid.*, 885.
162. *Ibid.*, 886.
163. *Ibid.*, 887.
164. *Ibid.*, 899.
165. *Ibid.*, 2419.
166. *Ibid.*, 890-c, 896, 900, 903.

167. *Ibid.*, 2419.
168. *Ibid.*, 890, a, b; 892, 892 a-g, 898, 893, 897.
169. *Ibid.*, 889, 891, 894, 898 a-c-, 901, 904, a-d; 902.

# CHAPTER II

# POLITICAL THOUGHT

The political thought of the early medieval dynasties of Central India may be best approached by understanding the Nature, the End and the Functions of the State and the Nature of Kingship as conceived and depicted in the inscriptions and literaray works of the times of the respective dynasties.

## THE CONCEPT OF STATE

### The Nature and End of the State

Ancient Indian political thinkers regarded the State as an organised whole. This Organic or Organism theory of the State can be studied mainly from two points of views *viz.* (i) that of the component parts of the Society and, (ii) that of the constituent elements of the State. From the former point of view, the Society was constituted by four orders (*varṇa*) *viz.* the Brāhmaṇa, the Kṣatriya, the Vaiśya and the Śūdra. All these elements are interdependent and work for the common good of man *viz.* the promotion of Dharma so that ultimately the individual is merged into the Society. From the latter point of view, the State (rājya) or body politic consists of seven limbs (*aṅgas*) technically called *Prakṛtis.* They are: *Svāmī* (the sovereign), *Amātya* (the Ministers and High officials of the State), *Janapada* or *Rāṣṭra* (territory or people), *Durga* (fort), *Kośa* (treasury or exchequer), *Daṇḍa* or *Bala* (army) and *Mitra* (allies). This doctrine of *Saptāṅga* is the epitome of the Hindu political constitution and several ancient Indian authorities have referred to it.[1] The End of the State has been recognised to be the promotion of four *Puruṣārthas, viz. Dharma, Artha, Kāma* and *Mokṣa.*

That the political thinkers of the early medieval dynasties of Central India were acquainted with the Nature and End of the State referred to above is shown by their available inscriptions. The Kartalai Stone Inscription of Kalachuri King Lakṣmaṇarāja of (K.) E. 593[2] and the Goharwa plates of Karṇa[3] refer to the *Varṇāśrama* ideal of the society. Similarly, the Abhona plates of Śaṅkaragaṇa of (K.) E. 347,[4] the Kharod Stone Inscription of Ratnadeva III of Cedi year 933[5]; and the Ratanpur Stone Inscription of Jājalladeva I[6] refer to the seven constituents of the State. Similarly, the Mau Stone inscription of Candella Kīrtivarman says that he had "defeated the host of enemies together with all the six internal enemies and day by day rendered more prosperous the seven constituent parts of the kingdom (*añjani sapta*) together with virtue."[7]

### The Functions of the State

The duty of the Hindu State has been summed up as 'Protection'. It has, however, been expanded into '*rakṣaṇa*' (protection), '*pālana*' (maintenance) and '*anurañjana*' (recreation) in the works on ancient Indian politics. The term 'protection' according to Hindu view, is not merely negative-a mere 'hindrance of hindrances', but positive which comprises the whole of life: political, economic, religious and cultural. From the political point of view, 'protection' means the defence of the territory from the external enemies and internal chaos and maintenance of law and order in the country. From the religious point of view, the State protects religion and morality, the customs and traditions and administers justice. From the economic point of view, the term means protection of the people from natural calamities like flood, earthquake, disease, famine, fire etc. From cultural point of view, it implies promotion of art, education and learning.

Ancient Hindu political thought prescribed that the King being the head of the State, had to look after all these aspects of life. As discussed below,[8] the same is reflected in the inscriptions of the early medieval dynasties of Central India also.

## THE NATURE OF KINGSHIP

### The Divine Theory

Some statements in the inscriptions of the Kalachuris indicate vaguely that kings regarded themselves as men born with divinity. Most of the inscriptions refer to the kings as *deva,* some as *Sākṣātaparameśvara,*[9] while others, as *nareśvara.*[10] The Banaras Plates of Karṇa refer to the divine personality of the king.[11] The Pujaripali Stone Inscription of Gopāladeva refers to him as the son of Goddess Vārāhī. Inscriptions of the Paramāras and Candellas often refer to their rulers as '*Parameśvara*'. All these had, however, nothing to do with the Divine Theory of Kings promulgated in some of our law books.

There is not a single instance in the history of the early medieval dynasties of Central India to prove that these eulogies of the panegyrists were taken with any seriousness. This is further evidenced by the limitations imposed on the authority of the king, some of which are as follow.

**Limitations of King's Authority**

Firstly, the King was not the law-maker. The Laws (sacred laws), according to the Hindu political conception, are co-eval with social organisation and they cannot be altered, changed or modified by any secular power. The King as the head of the State was only to obey, support and execute them and to that extent his powers were restricted.

Secondly, according to Hindu political theory, the State consists of seven *prakṛtis* or constituent elements *viz.* the King (*svāmī*), Minister (*amātya*), Territory (*rāṣtra*), Fort (*durga*), Treasury (*kośa*), Army (*daṇḍa*) and the Ally (*mitra*) and as we have seen above, this is recognized in the inscriptions of the Kalachuris[12] and other contemporary dynasties of the time. The King was, thus, only one of the seven elements of the State and not outside it. It means that though he might have been most important, he was not the absolute.

Thirdly, the Ministry, which comprised the second of the seven elements of the State had a considerable influence upon the King. Though the ministers were appointed by the King, the King had to follow a definite pattern of administration in consultation with the ministers and under the guidance of the *Rājaguru* and to that extent his powers were limited.

Fourthly, there were certain self-governing and autonomous bodies like *Śreṇis* (guilds), and *gaṇas* (corporations) in existence. The local administration was carried out with the guidance of the *Pañcakulas.* The existence of these institutions must have exercised wholesome influence on the despotic tendencies of the Kings.

Fifthly, the *Sāmantas* (feudatories); a considerable number of whom existed within the Kalachuri empire, enjoyed certain rights and privileges. Much freedom was given to them within the limits of their jurisdiction. To the extent these feudatories enjoyed these rights, the absolutism of the king was under restraint.

Sixthly, the discipline under which the princess of the time were educated must have put a great restraint over the despotic activities of the kings. We will see how, in their attempt to attain the ideals of physical, moral and intellectual qualities, the rulers of the time tried to become benevolent rulers. The ideals of life set before them was thus a great boon in keeping their despotic tendencies under control.

Lastly, it may be asked, if there was any institutional relation between the King and his subjects. As far as the Hindu political theory is concerned, no such relationship has been defined. The only bond that brought them closer was the parental feeling which the ruler had toward his subjects and the filial affection and regard that the subjects had for their king. That the rulers of the Kalachuri dynasty tried to attain this ideal is reflected in the Kharod Stone Inscription of Ratnadeva III of Cedi year 933 according to which Jājalladeva II was to the people like their own father.[13] It reminds one of the ideal of "All men are my children" enunciated by Aśoka in his edicts. Such a king was naturally "always dear to the people as one who made them happy".[14] Such sentiments are often reflected in the inscriptions of the Paramāras of Malwa and the Candellas of Jejākabhukti also. These will be discussed in detail below under the duties of the king.

## REFERENCES

1. For details, see Kane, P.V. : *History of Dharmaśāstra*, vol. III (1946), p. 17.
2. Mirashi, V.V. : *CII*, IV, Ins. no. 37, line 1.
3. *Ibid.*, Ins. no. 50 verse 28.
4. *Ibid.*, Ins. no. 12 line 6.
5. *Ibid.*, Ins. no. 100 verse 25.
6. *Ibid.*, Ins. no. 77 verse 22.
7. *EI*, vol. I, p. 198, vs 8.
8. See : Duties of King.
9. *Ibid.*, Ins. no. 48 verses 16 and 50 verse 12.
10. *Ibid.*, Ins. no. 66.
11. *Ibid.*, Ins. no. 48 verse 26.
12. *CII*, IV, Ins. nos. 100 verse 25; 66 line 7 and 77 verse 22.
13. *Ibid.*, Ins. no. 100 verse 11.
14. *Ibid.*, Ins. no. 83 verse 4.

# CHAPTER III

# ADMINISTRATIVE ORGANISATION

In the light of the ancient Hindu political thought outlined above, the administrative organization of Central India during the early medieval period may be best understood by discussing in detail each of the seven limbs *(aṅgas)* as conceived in the inscriptions and other evidences related to the period concerned.

## THE KING

The monarchy, during the period concerned, was hereditary and generally the law of primogeniture prevailed. Usually, the eldest son by the Chief Queen succeeded to the throne and his accession was secured by his nomination as the *Yuvarāja* or the crown-prince even during the life time of king, and his association with administration: Ample evidence of this is found in the inscriptions of the Kalachuris. The Tewar stone inscription of Gayākarṇa dtd (K) E. 902, referring to the association of the crown prince with the administration says "May the illustrious king Gayākarṇa together with his son the crown prince Narasiṁha, rule the earth as long as the world will endure".[1] The crown prince was called *Yuvarāja,*[2] *Mahārājaputra*[3] or *Mahākumāra.*[4] Junior princes were often appointed to govern outlying provinces. Thus, Kokalladeva I had eighteen sons of whom, the eldest succeeded to the throne and the younger ones were appointed rulers of the neighbouring *maṇḍalas.*[5] If a king had no son, usually, the choice fell on younger brother. The Kahla Plates of Soḍhadeva states that Lakṣmaṇarāja was placed on the throne by his eldest brother.[6] Bālahara was similarly succeeded by his younger brother Yuvarājadeva I. Similar was the case with Śaṁkaragaṇa III and Narasiṁha who were succeeded by Yuvarājadeva II and Jayasiṁha respectively. The same is reflected in the history of the Kalachuris of Kalyāṇa also. In case of the Candellas, two such instances are there of Vijayaśakti and Kīrtivarman. In case a king died leaving behind a prince who was minor, the young prince was appointed as king. This is clear from the Khairha and Jabalpur plates of Yaśaḥkarṇa which state that "the Chief Ministers of the lord of the earth placed on the throne, his (*i.e.* Yuvarājadeva II's) son Kokalla II, a lion-like prince."[7] Similarly, from the Pendrabandh Plates of Pratāpamalla, we come to know that Pratāpamalla was placed on the throne while quite young.[8] Since it is not possible for a young prince to carry on the heavy responsibilities of the administration, it seems that the Government was carried on by a Regency Council who did everything in the name and on behalf of the ward. We find the same situation reflected in the case of the Candellas. The legendary *Parmal Raso* quotes the case of Paramardi who was only a boy of five when he was called upon to succeed his father.[9] In inscriptions also he is called "*balopineta*".[10] Nothing is known about the Regency Council to conduct the administration. There is no evidence to show that there were cases of disputed succession. Thus, the Paramāra ruler Vākpati II made his nephew Bhoja his *Yuvarāja*, though his younger brother was alive. *Mahākumāra* Lakṣmīvarman's principality was inherited by his grandson Udayavarman, though his son Hariścandra was alive. If the king died in the battlefield without leaving any male issue, his nearest relative could claim the thrown as in case of Paramāra Jayasiṁha I, the successor of Bhoja.

In the inscriptions of the Candellas, there is reference to the ritual of coronation ceremony (*mūrddhābhiṣikta*)[11] which a new king had to pass through on his accession to the throne. Details are not indicated in any of the records. But the signs of royalty, as referred to different inscriptions are *siṁhāsana*[12] (throne), *pādapīṭha* (foot stool)[13], *ātapatra* (royal umbrella)[14], *mauli* (head-garland or the crown),[15] etc. These indicate that the usual splendour and majesty were associated with the royal office of the Candellas. There are references also to the royal retinue and the royal palace.

More such references are available in the inscriptions of the Kalachuri rulers.

The Jabalpur Plates of Jayasiṁha of (K) E. 918[16] and the Banares Plates of Karṇa of (K) E. 793[17] simply state that on hearing the coronation of king Jayasiṁha and Karṇa, respectively, their enemies disappeared. Of the central rite of *abhiṣeka* which consisted of pouring sacred water on king's head, the Kahla Plates of Soḍhadeva states that "Bhīma had his beautiful person bathed (at the time of his coronation) with the auspicious waters (poured) from the jars."[18] That such a ceremony was "guided by the family priest" is indicated in the Khairha Plates of Yaśaḥkarṇa of (K) E. 823.[19] Regarding the age of coronation, there seems to have been no restriction. We have already noted above that kings came to throne even when quite young. That the king in the case of abdication himself crowned his son is referred to in the Khairha Plates of Yaśaḥkarṇa of (K) E. 823 which state that "of this pious prince ( *i.e.* Yaśaḥkarṇa the father (*i.e.* Karṇa), whose actions were pure, performed himself the great coronation, ceremony."[20] Successful completion of war was sometimes celebrated by a special coronation. This is known in case of Karṇa, who, to proclaim his attainment of the position of *Cakravartin* performed his second coronation in the (K) E. 804 (1052-53 A.D.). His regnal year mentioned in the Rewa. Stone inscription of his general Vappulla[21] is counted from this second coronation.

Regarding abdication of throne, two cases are known in the history of the Candellas. The Khajuraho record of V.S. 1059[22] and a Kalanjar record[23] refer to voluntary abdication of throne by Dhaṅga and Jayavarman respectively. Siyaka II, the Paramāra ruler of Malwa abdicated his throne in favour of his heir apartment Vākpati II. However, more such cases are noticeable in case of the rulers of the Kalachuris.

To quote an instance, Kalachuri Karṇa abdicated throne in favour of his son Yaśaḥkarṇa and retired in his old age from active politics. That such abdications were done by kings for their younger brothers also, is shown by two instances in the history of the Kalachuris. That king Jagaddeva or Ratanpur branch probably relinquished his claim to the throne for his younger brother Jājalladeva II and himself went to fight with the Eastern Gaṅgās, is suggested in the Kharod inscription of Ratnadeva III of Cedi year 933. When, however, there was disorder in the country, probably after the death of Jājalladeva II, he returned home hastily and established peace and order. A similar instance of abdication was with Ullabha of the Sarayupāra branch of the Kalachuris who abdicated the throne if favour of his younger brother Bhāmāna I. Bijjala of the Kalyāṇa branch of the Kalachuris also did the same.

The sovereignty of a monarch is expressed symbolically in the form of titles. In case of the Kalachuris, we find that *Mahārājādhirāja* was the common title used by most of the kings. There is conspicuous absence of high sounding titles in case of early Kalachuri kings. Śaṅkaragaṇa I used the titles of *Paramabhaṭṭārka Mahārājādhirāja* and *Parameśvara,*[24] Yuvarājadeva probably *Trikaliṅgādhipati* [25] only and Gāṅgyadeva, *Mahārha-mahāmahattaka Mahārāja";*[26] probably also *Trikaliṅgādhipati.*[27] It was at the time of Karṇa, the greatest king of the Kalachuri dynasty that the tradition of using high-sounding titles was started which continued to be used by the later kings of the dynasty throughout its history. In his Banaras Plates of (K) E. 193 Karṇa uses the titles of *Paramabhaṭṭāraka Mahārājādhirāja Parmeśvara Paramamāheśvara* and *Trikaliṅgādhipati.*[28] We find this title expanded in his Goharwa Plates[29] and later record which refer to him as *Paramabhaṭṭāraka Mahārājādhirāja Parmeśvara Paramamāheśvara, Trikaliṅgādhipati, Nijabhujopārjit-āśvapati-gajapati-narapati-rāja-tray-ādhipatya i.e.*, who by his arms has acquired overloadship over three types of *rājās viz.* the lord of horses, the lord of elephants and the lord of men. The two different stages of the expansion of the titles of Karṇa probably indicate the two different stages of the expansion of his empire and this is evidenced by historical facts. The first record noted above belongs to the first seven years of Karṇa's reign during which he attained remarkable victories in the East, South and West. Later inscriptions belonged to the period of his reign after he had attained the height of his power holding practically the whole of Central India, and exercised his influence over North, South, East and West.

Apart from these imperial titles, the kings used special personal titles *(birudas)*. Thus, Kokalla I's son and successor Śaṅkaragaṇa II adopted three *birudas viz. Mugdhatuṅga, Prasiddhadhavala* and *Raṇavigraha.* Similarly, Bālaharṣa was probably the *biruda* of Śaṅkaragaṇa II's successor, whose personal name is not known.

The influence of the Kalachuris whom the Candella rulers defeated, is noticed in the adoption of the *Gaja-Lakṣmī* emblem on the latter's seals and coins. To the same influence was due the assumption of the well-known Kalachuri titles by some of Candella rulers, *viz.*, "*Parama-Māheśvara Srīmad Vāmadevapādanudhyāta*", and "*Trikaliṅgādhipati nijabhujopārjit-āśvapati-gajapati-nārapati rājatrayādhipati*", pre fixed to the name of Candella. Trailokyavarman in the Rewa copper plate of Kumārapāla.[30] The Dhureti copper plate[31] issued shortly. After the conquest of Rewa area by Trailokyavarman also reveals that, besides the Kalachuri titles, some titles of the Gāhaḍavāla rulers *viz.*, *'Paramabhaṭṭāraketyādi -samasta rājāvalīvirājamāna'* (The king endowed with all the royal titles, commencing with *Paramabhaṭṭāraka*'), '*Vividha-vidyā-vicharavācaspati*' (expert like a *Vācaspati* or *Bṛhaspati* in the pursuit of different sciences) and '*Kānya-kubjādhipati*'(lord of Kānyakubja), were used with the name of the Candella king. Some of the titles are specially significant. The description of king as "*vividhavidyā vichāra-vācaspati*" proves that he must have been acquainted with the sciences studied in his time which led to the sharpening of his intellect and development of his power of judgment. A *sati* record of the time of Hammīravarman (1308 A.D.)[32] and the Charkhari Copper Plate of Hammīravarman (1346 V.S.)[33] also use the title '*rājāvalītrayopeta*' for the ruler, evidently implying '*aśvapati*', '*gajapati*', and '*narapati*'. In L 12 of the Dhureti Copper Plate Trailokyavarman is given the epithet, '*Triśatīrājyādhipati*' (the lord of the kingdom consisting of three hundred), which is not met with elsewhere.[34]

The case of the Paramāra rulers of Malwa is slightly different. Early Paramāra rulers used simple title like *Mahārāja, Nṛpa* and *Bhūpa* as they were feudatories. From Vākpati II onwards the imperial titles used by them were *Paramabhaṭṭāraka Mahārājadhirāja* and *Parmeśvara.* Other epithets used by them were *Śrīvallabha, Pṛthvīvallabha* and *Amoghavarṣa* of the Rāṣṭrakūṭas. Vākpati II took the title of *Kavibāndhava* as he was a patron of poets. Sindhurāja has the title *Navasāhasāṅka* and Bhoja was called *Sarvabhauma Cakravartin, Tribhuvana-nārāyaṇa, siṣṭa-śiromani* and *Sarasvati-Kaṇṭhābharaṇa.* Naravarman took pride in calling himself *Nirvāṇa-Nārāyaṇa.*

The duties and functions of the kings are often referred to in the contemporary epigraphical records. They may be clarified from the point of view of Politics and Administration, Religion and Art, Education and learning.

Regarding the Political and Administrative duties of the king, the contemporary inscriptions show that the first and the foremost duty of the King was of political and administrative nature. As the head of the administrative machinery, his authority was supreme. He appointed Viceroys, Ministers, Governors and military officers and transferred them according to his will. He conferred titles and other distinctions such as *Pañca-mahā-śabda* for meritorious service. He was the Commander-in-Chief of the army and the Supreme Judge of the country. Protection of life and property of his subject, and looking for their general well-being engaged his attention. The Ratanpur Stone Inscription of Vāhara of (V) E. 1552 states that he (Vāhara) was "a unique king in respect of protection of the earth".[35] The Raipur Plates of Pṛthvīdeva I of (K) E. 821, similarly states that "while he who is strong in political insight in protecting the earth, even wind does not take to the wrong path", resulting from which "there is indeed no out-break of even the slightest divine calamity".[36] With such strong administration under the Kalachuri kings "thieves disappeared, obstacles (vanished), dangers departed, the enemies took shelter in the corners of mountain-caves (and) the people roaming in dense forests had no fear even from a tiger.[37] Such a King "who was a store of valour and the sole resource of (their) happiness dwelt in the mind of (his) subjects, their inward distress completely disappeared.".[38] Such Kings have been rightly described in the Kalachuri inscriptions as "protector of the earth"[39], "supporter of the world"[40] and "the sole source of the happiness of the world."[41] The picture of the country in absence of such a protection from the king has been vividly described in the Sheorinarayan Stone inscription of Jājalladeva II of Cedi year 919 in which it is stated that after the death of Jājalladeva "beauty vanished, life departed, charity left for (distant) regions, prowess knew no judicious habitation, playful actions stayed far away, merits became religious mendicants."[42]

Allied to the duty of the King to provide for security of life and property was his more important duty of the protection of his subjects from injustice and social anarchy.

King's concern in affording protection to the people against internal and external dangers is best evident from the description of the state as *"kulavadhu"* (*kulavadhūmiva vasundharārṁ nirākulaṁ paripālayannavikala viveka nirmalikṛtamati...*) referred in the inscriptions of the Candellas. This conception is evidently based on the idea that a state is, like a wife, depending entirely on the husband for the protection of her person and honour. As it is the sacred duty of the husband to protect her, so also is the duty of the king to protect his subjects, who are helpless like a wife and should be defended by the king.

Epithets like *parā-rakṣā bhūteṣvapi'* (carefully protecting all beings-Mau Ins., V. 13), *'trasta-trāṇa-praguaṇ-manasāṁ'* (Khajuraho Ins, V. 9), '*hṛdi prajānām-ātaṅkaśaṅikuṁ*' (weapon to destroy fear from the hearts of the subjects, (Khajuraho Ins., IV., V. 17), etc., indicate that the Candella rulers were particularly careful in the matter of maintenance of the security of their kingdom. The period was full of troubles and dangers. There were not only external dangers, evil forces were also at work within the

Candella territory. The people were afraid of dire calamities threatening them from all sides. A striking emphasis is therefore placed on the king's power to remove terror from their minds.

There are numerous references in the Candella records to the 'weeding out of thorns' -'*kṛtya kaṇṭaka Śodhanaṁ janapade*'– (Mau Record, V. 39); "*ucchinnaḥ kaṇṭakaugha*' (Mau Record, V. 8); '*dūrādhaḥ kṛta kaṇṭakasya*'(Batesvar Ins., V. 24; '*sphītaṁ rājyaṁ akaṇṭakaṁ*'— (Rock Insc. of Bhojavarman, V.20); '*kṣapita nikhila duṣṭaḥ*' (Mau Record, V. 6); and '*duṣṭaprahantā*' (Rock Insc. of Vīravarman, V.9) *i.e.*, extermination of the wicked and subversive elements from the kingdom. These references show that the Candella rulers were alert and watchful, and they took stern steps to exterminate all elements of disorder.

Another serious and very responsible administrative function which fell on the king was to formulate a sound foreign policy. Every king of the early medieval dynasties of Central India was a soldier-statesman. Imbibed with the ideal of '*digvijaya*'; the imperial Kalachuri rulers launched on the career of conquests. This was with the Paramāra and Candella rulers also. Kings like Gāṅgeyadeva and Karṇa acquired honoured titles of universal paramountcy of *Vikramāditya* and *Cakravartin* and their titles were no idle boasts. To achieve their objectives, that they were well acquainted with the four well-known traditional measures of *Sāma, Dāma, Daṇḍa* and *Bheda,* is reflected in the Karanbel Stone Inscription of Jayasiṁha which states that "he (Yaśaḥkarṇa) clever and adept in policy as he was, achieved the four desired objects of life with the four well-known measures used in their respective spheres."[43] Some wars waged by the kings were defensive in character and others offensive. All the same, it was the duty of the king to see that vigorous policy was pursued in matters of foreign relationship.

More important than these duties of the King was the preservation of the social solidarity of the people by enforcing on them the observance of the *Ārya-Dharma* based on the time-immemorial customs and the authority by the Sacred Texts. Society according to the Hindus, exists for the maintenance of *Dharma, i.e.* the doing of that which is good and conducive to the attainment of the ultimate object of existence. The State is embodied in the Society to enable those constituting the Society to pursue this *Dharma* unhampered by those with whom their lot in life may be cast. The ideal of *Dharma* provides the motive for social life, and the duty of a government, as an organ of society, is to provide for the undisturbed maintenance of *Dharma* on the earth. In order to do it, it must establish the social orders *(varṇa)* and the stations in life's progress (*āśramas*). According to Manu, "the king has been created (to be) the protector of classes (*varṇa*) and orders, who, all according to their rank, discharge their social duties."[44] During the period of our study, the Hindu society was based, as it still continues to be, on the *Varṇāśrama* ideal. The fact that in the opening verse of the Karitalai stone inscription of Lakṣmaṇarāja I of (K) E. 593[45] reverence is paid to the *Cmaturvarṇa* along with Brahmā, Viṣṇu and Śiva, indicates the sanctity which was attached to the ideal of the four *varṇas* in the Society. Reference to the four, *āśramas* is found in the Goharwa Plates of Karṇa.[46]

The kings of the period like other Hindu kings in the past, always thought that the protection of the religion of the people was one of their most important functions. Their activity in this direction is well borne out by the title of *Paramamāheśvara* which most of the Kalachuri kings bore. It indicates that they were wedded to the cult of Śiva. The use of other religious titles like *Paramavaiṣṇava* and *Bhaṭṭārakaprabha* has already been noticed above. The kings took a very broad and tolerant view with regard to patronage to religion and this is evidenced by the fact that the cults of Brahmā, Viṣṇu, Śiva, Buddha, Jaina, Śakti, and Sun etc. were flourishing simultaneously throughout the dominion of the respective dynasties. Another aspect in which the interest of the kings in the religion of the land is reflected, is in the intense donative and building activities in the interest of the promotion of religion. The inscriptions indicate that the kings had belief in the *mahādānas* like *Tulāpuruṣa.*[47] Besides this, land in villages nad sometimes even whole villages were given in grant to individuals and institutions for the promotion of learning and religious teachings. Above all, the inscriptions of the period are full of references to many temples, monasteries and places of religious worship which the kings caused to be constructed for the promotion of religious learning. As promoters of ancient traditions, the kings themselves undertook pilgrimages to holy shrines and waters and participated in religious festivals. All these efforts on the part of the kings "increased the legs of *Dharma*" as the Karanbel Stone Inscriptions of Jayasiṁha points out.[48]

Promotion of Art, Education and Learning are a test of any civilization and in this respect they took abiding interest in the advancement of arts, especially fine arts. Huge temples going even upto 12 or 16 stories were constructed by them at different centres. In point of architecture and sculpture that they were superb is still indicated by the extant remains of many of them. The rulers thought it to be their most important duty to promote education and learning. A great impetus was given to Sanskrit and Prakrit by giving patronage to poets of eminence. All these gave a rare outburst of the literary activities and we find a reflection of it in the ornate *Kāvya* style embellished with *arthālaṅkāras* of the *praśastis* of the kings of the different dynasties of the period.

## THE MINISTERS

The Hindu doctrine of *Saptāṅga* recognizes Minister (*amātya*) as the second of the seven elements of the state. Since the State and the Governments, during the early medieval period of Central India followed the doctrine of *Saptāṅga*, the acceptance of Minister as the second *aṅga* of the state is clear. Infact, in Hindu political thought a king is supposed to be endowed with three political powers *viz. Prabhu Śakti* (power by army and treasure), *Mantra Śakti* (power due to good counselling) and *Utsāha Śakti* (personal valour). Reference of *Mantra Śakti* appears in some of the inscriptions of the Kalachuris.[49]

Appointment of a minister was done by the king and many were the considerations before him for the selection. The principle of heredity was one of the major considerations before him. Ancient Indian works like *Manusmṛti*,[50] *Śukrarīti*,[51] *Rāmāyaṇa*,[52] *Agnipurāṇa*,[53] *Matsyapurāṇa*[54] and *Viṣṇudharmottarapurāṇa*[55] etc.

prescribed that ministership was to be heredity if the son was capable like his father. That the principle was practiced by the Kalachuris is evidenced by several instances. The Koni Stone Inscription of Pṛthvīdeva II of (K) E. 900 states[56] that Brāhmaṇa Soḍhadeva obtained hereditary ministership of Pṛthvīdeva and that he belonged to a family which served the Kalachuri princes for several generations. The same inscription points out that his grandson Puruṣottama was appointed to the post of *Sarvādhikārin* (minister plenipotentiary) by Ratnadeva III. A similar instance of hereditary ministership is indicated in the Rewa Stone Inscription of Vijayasiṁha of (K) E. 944[57] which traces the pedigree of Malayasiṁha, a feudatory chief of the king. The first ancestor of Malayasiṁha named in the inscription is Jāṭa who was appointed as the head of a *Viṣaya* by Karṇa. His son was Yaśaḥpāla who was devoted Councillor of Gayākarṇa. He had two sons Padmasiṁha and Candrasiṁha, of whom the latter became the pre-eminent Home Minister of the Cedi king Vijayasiṁha. Padmasiṁha had a son named Kīrtisiṁha who was the father of Malayasiṁha. A similar instance of hereditary ministership is noticed in case of Someśvara the son of Bhākamiśra in the Karitalai Stone Inscription of Lakṣmaṇarāja II.[58]

In the history of the Candellas, the practice of hereditary succession to ministerial posts may be noted in the genealogy of two families of ministers who worked under different Candella Kings. Reference to these appear in the Mau stone inscriptions of Madanavarman[59] and Baghari stone inscription of Paramardi.[60] The former refers to Prabhāsa, Śivaṅga, Mahipāla, Ananta, Yogeśvara, Gadādhara, Vāmana and Pradhumna who served as ministers during the reigns of Dhaṅga, Gaṇḍa, Vidyādhara, Vijayapāla, Kīrtivarman, Jayavarman, Pṛthvīvarman and Madanavarman. The second list mentions Lahaḍa and his successors as ministers during the regime of different rulers.

The principle of heredity, though important, was not the only consideration. The principle that one should not be appointed to a high office without proved efficiency, even though born in a family of ministers, was apparently followed by the Kalachuri kings. This is shown in case of the successors of Malayasiṁha whose instance of hereditary ministership has been quoted above. Thus, verse 27 of the Koni Stone Inscription states that Puruṣottama the *Sarvādhikārin* of Ratnadeva had four sons Madhusūdana, Lakṣmīdhara, Yaśodhara and Gaṅgādhara, all of whom turned out to be able statement and the eldest of them Madhusūdana attained great renown. Omission of any specific title with their names indicates that even the eldest of them did not succeed his father as *Sarvādhikārin* but at the most, as a minister. This is further evidenced by the Ratanpur Stone Inscription of Pṛthvīdeva II of (K) E. 915,[61] according to which, Pṛthvīdeva's *Sarvādhikārin* was his *Mandalika* Brahmadeva whom he specially called from *Talāhari-maṇḍala* and made his Chief Minister. A similar instance may be noticed in case of the sons of Gaṅgādhara the Prime Minister of Ratnadeva III.[62] If may thus be said that the advantage of birth was no the only qualification that was considered in the appointment of ministers by the Kalachuri kings.

Caste, like heredity, proved no barrier in the selection of ministers. According to most of the ancient Indian authorities on polity, the *mantrins* should be chosen from among the Brāhmaṇas, the Kṣatriyas and the Vaiśyas, but not from the Śūdras even if the latter be endowed with all qualities. That this practice was followed by the Kalachuri kings, is proved in several instances. Among the prominent Brāhmaṇa ministers of the Kalachuri court, mention may be made of Bhākamiśra (the Prime Minister of Yuvarājadeva I) and his son Someśvara (the Prime Minister of Lakṣmaṇarāja II)[63], Soḍhadeva (the minister of Pṛthvīdeva) I and his successors.[64]

Gaṅgādhara (the Prime Minister Ratnadeva I)[65] etc. Malayasimha and his predecessors were all Kṣatriyas,[66] Vallabharāja whose ancestors were ministers of the Kalachuri kings was a Vaiśya[67] and Someśvara of the Rewa Stone Inscription of (K) E. 800,[68] belonged to the family of the Kāyasthas. No instance of Śūdra minister comes to our knowledge from the study of the Kalachuri Inscriptions.

What then were the specific qualifications that the Kalachuri kings expected of their ministers? The qualifications of ministers are laid down at several places in ancient Indian literature.[69] In the opinion of Kauṭilya whose views were later endorsed in a varied degree by Kāmandaka and Śukra, a minister should be expected to be endowed with twenty five personal qualifications and attainments. How far the ministers possessed these qualifications can be known from the fragments of information about them that are available in the inscriptions of the different dynasties ruling over Central India during the period concerned.

All writers on Hindu political philosophy have observed that a king in order to decide as to who, on account of the possession of the above mentioned qualifications, should be selected for ministership should apply the four-fold test of honesty, known in the *Arthaśāstra* and *Nītisāras* as *Upadhā*. They are, as it were secret tricks applied to these persons by the king through various agencies, spies and others for testing their honesty. These *Upadhās* are four-fold *viz.* (1) *Dharmopadhā* or ethical allurements; (2) *Arthopadhā; i.e.* pecuniary allurements (3) *Kāmopadhā i.e.* carnal allurements; and (4) *Bhayaopadhā, i.e.* frightful or dreadful allurements. Unless a candidate for ministership is proved to be *Upadhā*-proof in respect of all these four kinds of allurements, kings never appointed him as minister. That this practice was continued by the Kalachuri administration also is testified by the Koni Stone Inscription of Pṛthvīdeva II of (K) E. 900, which states that the good character of Puruṣottama was testified by all kinds of tests before he was offered the post of Sarvādhākrin by Ratnadeva II.[70] Practical application of these tests in case of appointments of several ministers by the Candella rulers may be noticed in several instances.

In ancient Indian literature often no distinction is made between the three terms *viz. Amātya, Saciva* and *Mantrin*. However, some distinctions are sometimes made by Kauṭilya, Amarasiṁha and the Buddhist lexicographer of the Gupta period. Dr. Kane's view is that the terms *Mantrin, Saciva* and *Amātya* are usually interchangeable though sometimes distinguishable[71] seems applicable to the administrative organization of Central India during the early medieval period. These three titles have frequently been used in the inscriptions of the different dynasties and the duties and qualifications associated with their bearers indicate little difference among them.

As regards the strength of the ministry is concerned, divergent views were held by the authors of the *Smṛtis* and *Arthaśāstra*. Manu holds that the ministry should consist of 7 or 8 members,[72] the latter number is prescribed by the *Mahābhārata*.[73] *Arthaśāstra* quotes different views from which we learn that the *Mānava*, *Bārhaspatya* and the *Auśanas* schools were in favour of a ministry of 12, 16 and 20 respectively.[74] The *Śukranīti*[75] records a ministry of ten and the *Nītivākyāmṛta* is in favour of a smaller ministry of 3, 5, or 7 members only. The difference of opinion on the question is due to the different needs of the different states and at different times. Manu[76] and Kauṭilya[77] agree in stating that the actual number of ministers should depend on the needs of the situation in the state concerned. It is the view which seems to have been practiced in the administration of the different states of Central India during early medieval period. The varying lists together with the varying chronological sequence of functionaries of the state appearing in the inscriptions of the dynasties can only be explained by the fact that the strength of the ministers differed from time to time according to needs.

Each of the ministers was in charge of a portfolio over which king seems to have kept a close watch. Sometimes, there were changes in the portfolios of the ministers and this is glaringly indicated in some of the inscriptions. This was in full agreement with the advise given by some of the ancient Indian authorities like Śukra.[78]

## REFERENCES


1. *CII*, IV, Ins. no. 58, v.4.
2. *Ibid.*
3. *Ibid.*, Ins. nos. 48 line 34; 50 line 35; 56 line 24; 61 line 6; 63 line 22; 74 line 34; Appendix 2 verse I etc.
4. *Ibid.*, Ins. no. 69 line1; Appendix 42 verse 27 etc.
5. *Ibid.*, Ins. nos. 76 verse 6; 77 verse 5.
6. *Ibid.*, Ins. no. 74 line 6.
7. *Ibid.*, Ins. no. 56 v 8 & 57.
8. *Ibid.*, Ins. no. 101 v 14.
9. *Parmal Raso,* II, v 108 p. 28.
10. *EI I*, p. 327, v, 6.
11. *Ibid.*, v 11.
12. *Ibid.*, p. 122, 1.9.
13. *Ibid.*, p. 209 v. 10.
14. *Ibid.*, p. 201, v. 42.
15. *Ibid.*, p.197, v. 5.
16. Mirashi, *CII,* IV, Ins. no. 63 v. 17.
17. *Ibid.*, Ins. no. 48 v. 28.
18. *Ibid.*, Ins. no. 74 v. 24.
19. *Ibid.*, Ins. no. 56 v. 16.
20. *Ibid.*, Ins. no. 56 v. 16.
21. *Ibid.*, Ins. no. 53 l.20.
22. *EI*, I, pp. 137-47 v. 55.
23. *JASB*, 1848, pt. I, pp. 318-19.
24. *Ibid*, Ins. no. 47, l.1.
25. *Viddhaśālabhañjikā* of Rājaśekhara, Act I, 39.
26. Mirashi, *CII.* IV., Ins. no. 47, line 1.
27. Mirashi, *CII.* IV, pt. I, p. xc.
28. *Ibid.*, Ins. no. 48, lines 33-34.
29. *Ibid.*, Ins. no. 50.
30. *IA*, VII, pp. 230-36.
31. *EI*, XXV, p. 2.

32. *Ibid.*, XVI, p. 10, fn. 4.
33. *Ibid.*, XX, pp. 134-35
34. *Ibid.*, XXV, p. 6.
35. *CII.* IV, Ins. nos. 103-4, v.1.
36. *CII.* IV, Ins. no. 75 v.2.
37. *Ibid.*, Ins. no. 100 v.14.
38. *CII.* IV, Ins. no. 50 verse 15.
39. *Ibid.*, Ins. no. 51 verse 33.
40. *Ibid.*, Ins. no. 74 verse 7.
41. *Ibid.*, Ins. no. 60 verse 8.
42. *Ibid.*, Ins. no. 98 verse 34.
43. *Ibid.*, Appdx. 3 verse 26.
44. *Manu*, IV. 176.
45. *Ibid.*, Ins. no. 37, line 1.
46. *Ibid.*, Ins. no. 50, verse 28.
47. *Manu*. IV. Ins no. 56 verse 21; Appdx. 3 verse 41.
48. *Ibid.*, Appdx. 3 verse 41.
49. *Ibid.*, Ins. no. 51, 12 line 6.
50. *Manu*, VII, 54.
51. *Śukra*, II, 114.
52. *Rāmāyaṇa*, II, 100, 26; *Mbh.* (*Sabhāparva* 5.43).
53. *Agnipurāṇa*, 220, 16-17.
54. *Matsyapurāṇa*, 215, 83-84.
55. *Viṣṇudharmottara*, II, 24, 53-56.
56. *Ibid.*, Ins. 90, verses 14-15.
57. *Viṣṇudharmottara*, II, Ins no. 90, verse 22-23.
58. *CII.* IV, Ins no. 42 verses 6-7.
59. *EI.I*, pp.199 ft.
60. *Ibid.*, pp. 207-14.
61. *CII*, IV, Ins. no. 96 line 20.
62. *Ibid.*, Ins. no. 100 verse 29.
63. *Viṣṇudharmottara*, II, Ins. no. 42 verse 2 and 7.
64. *CII.* IV., Ins. no. 90 verse 14.
65. *Ibid.*, Ins. no. 100 verse 26.

66. *Ibid.*, Ins.67 verses 43-46.
67. *Ibid.*, Ins. no. 67, verse 9.
68. *Ibid.*, Ins. no. 51 verse 46.
69. *Ibid.*, e.g. Kauṭilya, I. 9; Manu. VII. 54; *Kāmandaka Nītisāra*, IV. 23-30; *Yājñavalkasmṛti*, I,312; *Śāntiparva*, 118,2-3 and 80, 25-28; *Bālakāṇḍa*, 7.7-14; *Ayodhyākāṇḍa*, 100.15; *Medhātithi on Manu*,VII, 54; *Mānasollāsa*,11, 2, 52-59 etc.
70. *Viṣṇudharmottara*, II. Ins no. 90 verse 22-23.
71. Kane, P.V., *History of Hindu Dharmaśāstra*, vol. III, p. 104.
72. *Manu*, VII, 54.
73. *Mbh.*, XII, 85.
74. *Arthaśāstra*, BK.I, ch. 15.
75. *Śukranīti*, II, 70 .
76. *Manu*, VII, 61.
77. *Arthaśāstra*, BK I, ch 15.
78. *Śukranītisāra*, II, 107-13.

## CHAPTER IV

# HIGH OFFICIALS OF THE STATE

As per ancient Indian tradition which was in existence in theory and practice, the king used to issue his commands in presence of the high functionaries of the state. Thus, royal charters of the early medieval rulers of Central India furnish lists of high officials to whom the royal orders are addressed for compliance. The list generally furnished the names of the following officials:

**The Chief queen**

The status of the Chief Queen in the Kalachuri court, as depicted by the epigraphic evidences, was very sound. The inscriptions show that the Chief Queen had a definite place in the Kalachuri administration. In a number of land grants of the Kalachuris, of the customary lists of persons and officials who are made aware of each and every detail of the proposed endowment of land in which their formal consent is solicited, mention is made of *Mahārājñī* or *Mahādevī, i.e.* the Chief Queen. This shows that the Queen is duly informed of the condition, object and nature of the proposed grant and is cited among the witnesses who ratified the gift by her consent, whether tacit or express. The honourable position of the Chief

Queen is further reflected in the fact that sometimes while describing the genealogical accounts, the entire pedigree of the Chief Queen is traced. Thus, the Bilahari Stone Inscription of Yuvarājadeva II[1] describes the entire pedigree of Nohalā, the Chief Queen of Yuvarājadeva I, who was of the Cāḷukya lineage. We come across similar instance in the Bheraghat Stone Inscription of Narasiṁha of (K) E. 907[2] where the entire pedigree of Gayākarṇa's queen Alhaṇadevī, the daughter of Vijayasiṁha, is described. Evidence for the authoritative position of the Chief Queen is further strengthened by the fact of her being donor of monasteries, temples, lands and villages with or without referring to the permission obtained by the reigning king. Thus, though the Karitalai Stone Inscription of Lakṣmaṇarāja II, refers to the 'kings's consent'[3] obtained by the Queen Rāhaḍā for donating the village Chakrahradi, and similarly the Kumbhi Plates of Vijayasiṁha of (K) E. 932, refer to the grant of the village by the dowager queen Gosaladevī the mother of the king 'with our permission'[4] no such reference to permission is found in case of other records. Rather Śvetalladevī, the queen of Vallabharāja records in the Ratanpur Stone inscription of Pṛthvīdeva II of (K) E. 910 that she caused the construction of a tank 'of her own accord.'[5] Similarly, the Vadner Plates of Buddharāja of (K) E. 360, states that the record was written by the *Mahāsāndhivigrahādhikaraṇādhikṛta* (Chief Officer-in-charge of the Department of peace and War) at the request of the queen Anantamahāyī.[6] Several instances of political and religious influence of the Kalachuri queens are available in the Kalachuri inscriptions. Nohalā, the Chief Queen of Yuvarājadeva I greatly influenced the religious policy of her husband and invited to the Cedi country several ascetics of the Mattamayūra clan from her home country. She herself got built the lofty temple of Nohaleśvara and endowed it with gifts of several villages.[7] The dowager queen Alhanadevī also caused to be constructed a temple of Śiva, a monastery, a lecture-hall at Bheraghat and herself granted two villages for their maintenance. Similar is the case of Gosaladevī, who is mentioned prominently with her son and grandson in the Bheraghat Temple Inscription.[8] Upon her name was founded the city of Gosalapura. An interesting incident of political influence that the queen had over their sons is described in the Ratanpur Stone Inscription of Jājalladeva I of (K) E. 866, which states that Jājalladeva defeated Someśvara and imprisoned him with his ministers and wives, but afterwards released them as desired by his mother.[9] The Chief Queen had thus a very sound position in the Kalachuri administration.

### The Yuvarāja

The second important functionary, commonly found recorded in the official lists of the Kalachuri inscriptions is the *Yuvarāja*. Great emphasis is laid in the *Smṛtis* and the *Nītiśāstras* on the importance of the nomination of the *Yuvarāja* or the Crown Prince, to guard against the dangers of civil wars and usurpations.

According to *Śukranīti*, the Crown Prince is the head, the eye and the ear of a monarch.[10] The *Yuvarāja* was thus a part of the mechanism of the ancient Indian polity and we find the same reflected in the Kalachuri inscriptions also. As already noted above, the *Yuvarāja* is invariably found mentioned next to the Chief Queen in all the inscriptions of the Kalachuris which supply lists of officials.

The inscriptions used the terms *Yuvarāja, Mahārāja Kumāra, Mahākumāra* or simply *Kumāra* for the Crown-Prince. The fact that *Yuvarāja* is mentioned along with the kings implies that the nomination of the heir-apparent was done by the Kalachuri kings during their own life-time, evidently to destroy the possibility of any dispute with regard to succession to the throne after their own death. Conspicuously, we do not have any evidence of disputed succession in the history of the Kalachuris as evidenced by the Kalachuri inscriptions. As per ancient Indian tradition, the choice must have generally fallen upon the eldest son by the Chief Queen. Quite possibly, in case of absence of a son, such a choice used to fall upon the younger brother, the successor. The inscriptions of the Kalachuris are silent to indicate whether the selection of the *Yuvarāja* was done in consultation with or at least with the express knowledge of the ministers. But, the fact that the ministers were responsible for anointing Kokalla II, as indicated in the Khairha and Jabalpur Plates of Yaśaḥkarṇa, shows that the selection of the *Yuvarāja,* must have constitutional support of the king's ministers. There is no reference to the details of coronation of the *Yuvarāja* in Kalachuri inscriptions. During his boyhood, the *Yuvarāja* must have been kept under the care of able teachers to enable him to acquire the physical, moral and intellectual qualities required to become a successful ruler. On attaining maturity, he was usually associated with practical administration. While other princes were sent out as governors of provinces, the *Yuvarāja* was kept at the capital to help the king in administration and to succeed him. Several inscriptions of the Ratanpur branch state[11] that Kokalla had 18 sons, of whom the eldest became the lord of Tripuri and the younger brothers were made the lords of the *maṇḍalas*. The *Yuvarāja* took a prominent part in the wars of the reigning king. Thus, Śaṅkaragaṇa *alias* Mugdhatuṅga Prasiddhadhavala, as crown prince, was sent by his father Kokalla I to help his brother-in-law Rāṣṭrakūṭa Kṛṣṇa II in his war against the Eastern Cāḷukyas. Another son of Kokalla I, named Arjuna, seems to have helped Kṛṣṇa's son Jagattuṅga probably during his wars with the Gurjara Pratihāras. Similarly, Karṇa led an expedition against Magadha towards the close of the reign of his father Gāṅgeyadeva. He was probably obliged to patch-up as his presence at the capital was required by the approaching end of Gāṅgeyadeva.

It may thus be said that from the administrative point of view, the *Yuvarāja* occupied an important place in the Government. Constitutionally, his position was next to the king himself.

**Rājaguru**

*Rājaguru,* the spiritual preceptor of the Kalachuri kings exercised great influence in the administration. He was venerated by the kings and was consulted in important matters of the State. The statements of the Jabalpur Stone Inscription of Jayasiṁha of (K)E. 926 that Vimalaśiva, the *Rājaguru* of Jayasiṁha was 'always employed (by the king) in many suitable affairs[12] and that he showed great vigilances in looking after all royal affairs'[13] indicate that the *Rājagurus* were often entrusted with various kinds of works befitting their position. This is probably the reason why in the official records of the Kalachuri kings, he often finds place amongst the important functionaries of the State.[14]

The inscriptions of the Kalachuris mention several Śaiva- *ācāryas* who acted as *Rājagurus*. The Jabalpur Stone inscription of Jayasiṁha. (K) E. 926[15] supplies a list of *Rājagurus* of the Kalachuri kings from Yaśaḥkarṇa downwards upto his reign. According to the record, Puruṣaśiva was the *Rājaguru* of Yaśaḥkarṇa, Śaktiśiva of Gayākarṇa, Kīrtiśiva of Narasiṁha and Vimalaśiva of Jayasiṁha. The fact that Vimalaśiva is referred to as *Rājaguru* in the record of Vijayasiṁha,[16] the successor of Jayasiṁha, shows that he continued on the post, during the reign of both the kings. It seems that Vijayasiṁha, like his ancestor Yaśaḥkarṇa had two *Rājagurus* in succession. His Rewa Stone Inscription mentions his *Rājaguru* Vimalaśiva, whereas his Kumbhi Plates name *Śaivācārya Bhaṭṭāraka* Vidyādeva as his *Rājaguru*. Similar had once been the case with Yaśaḥkarṇa. The Asiatic Society of Bengal Plate of Govindacandra mentions[17] *Śaiva Ācārya* Rudraśiva as the *Rājaguru* of Yaśaḥkarṇa, whereas the Jabalpur Plates of Jayasiṁha refers to Puruṣaśiva as the *Rājaguru* of Yaśaḥkarṇa.

It is interesting to note that none of the inscriptions of the Ratanpur branch of the Kalachuris refer to *Rājaguru* among the functionaries of the State. Probably, inspite of the continuance of the post, he ceased to be considered a functionary of the State. His function in the ministry was probably performed by the minister - in-charge of the Department of Religion.

*Rājaguru* as a high functionary of the State was also in existence during the rule of the Paramāras of Malwa as we notice Madana as *Rājaguru* of Arjunavarman.

**Mahāmantrin (The Chief Councillor)**

The Chief among the Councillors is variously called in the Kalachuri inscriptions as '*Mahāmantrin Mantripradhāna*[18] and *Nītivinmantrakartāri.*[19] In the administration, he occupied a place next to that of the king. Reference to this high official is found in a number of Kalachuri inscriptions[20], some of them referring to them by name. Thus, the Karitalai Stone Inscription of Lakṣmaṇarāja refers to Someśvara who was the son of Bhākamiśra, the Chief Councillor(*mantripradhāna*) of Yuvarājadeva.[21] Similarly, the Rewa Stone Inscription of Vijayasiṁha of (K) E.96 (X)[22] refers to *Mahāmantrin* Haripāla. The Karitalai Stone Inscription highly eulogises Someśvara in eleven verses describing the physical, moral and intellectual qualities of the minister and in order to indicate the regard of the king for him, describes how once when his palanquin was about to fall owing to the exhausion of the bearer, the king Lakṣmaṇarāja himself put his shoulder to it.

**Mahāmātya (The Prime Minister)**

The *Mahāmātya* who was next in rank was also very powerful. In the inscriptions of Kalachuris, he is variously termed as *Pradhāna-Amātya,*[23] *Amātya-Mukhya,*[24] or simply as *Pradhāna.*[25] In the Koni Stone Inscription of Pṛthvīdeva II of (K) E. 900[26] he is called *Sarvādhikārin.* The term *Sarvādhikārin* has been used in the sense of the Prime Minister and not an officer different from the Prime Minister who was "sometimes appointed and invested with the supreme power of direction and administration" as supposed by Dr. Mirashi.[27] The term *Sarvādhikārin* has been used in the sense of Prime Minister in accordance firstly with *Śukranīti* which describes the Prime Minister as *Sarvadarśī-Pradhāna*[28], secondly, with a record from Halsi (of 6th century A.D.), in which the Prime Minister is called *Sarvasya Anuṣṭhātā*,[29] and thirdly, with a Yādava record which designates the Prime Minister of Yādava Kannara as *Sarvādhikārin*.[30]

The powerful position enjoyed by the Prime Minister is shown in the Kharod Stone Inscription of Ratnadeva III of (K) E. 933, which describes how disorganized state of affairs of his kingdom was restored to peace by following the policy of his Prime Minister Gaṅgādhara.[31] The Koni Stone Inscription of Pṛthvīdeva II states that multitude of princes were vanquished by the policy and prowess Prime Minister Puruṣottama so that Ratnadeva. II ruled without any trouble.[32] Owing to his exalted position, the Premier often enjoyed the status of the Chief Feudatory (*Māṇḍalika Agraṇi*) as we find in case of Brahmadeva during the reign of Pṛthvīdeva II.[33] A large number of the Kalachuri inscriptions refer to this official.[34]

**Mahāpradhāna**

In the administration of the Kalachuris this officer, the nature and function of whose position is not very clear in absence of sufficient data, seems to have been an officer different from *Mahāmātya* or *Mahāmantrin*. This is clearly indicated by the fact that at places in the lists of officers where these three officers are mentioned, they are shown on three different posts.[35] Some of the *Mahāpradhānas* of the administration of the Paramāras of Malwa where the Chief Ministers were so named were : Rudrāditya, the Chief Ministers of Vākpati II,

Puruṣottama of Yaśovarman and Ajayadeva and Chaduri of Jayavarman II.

**Mahāpurohita and Dharmapradhana**

*Mahāpurohita,* the Chief Priest played a role that was pre-eminently religious. By his prayers and requisite rituals (*purohitakarmas*) as recommended in the *Atharvaveda,* he was expected to propitiate gods and secure their help in warding off all calamities for the success of the King and his subjects. Gods, it was believed in ancient times, would not accept oblations of a king except from the *Purohita.* It is in this spirit that the Khairha Plates of Yaśaḥkarṇa state that Karṇa "whose actions were full, being guided by the family priest performed himself the great coronation ceremony" of Yaśaḥkarṇa.[36] As a member of the royal house-hold, therefore, the *Mahāpurohita* enjoyed a covetous position. The fact that he is mentioned in the Kalachuri inscriptions as one of the functionaries of the State, indicates his importance in the administration. The king was expected to consult him in all important State matters and his reputation exercised considerable influence in controlling arbitrary actions of the king.

During the earlier part of the regime of the later Kalachuris, *Mahāpurohita* was probably entrusted with the headship of the Department of Religion. The Khairha and the Jabalpur Plates of Yaśaḥkarṇa mention *Mahāpurohita* among the official witness of the royal orders. Since no other official is mentioned in these two records who is shown in any way connected with the Department of Religion, it seems that *Mahāpurohita* was looking after the department. During the reign of

Jayasiṁha and Vijayasiṁha, however, another official designated as *Dharmapradhāna* was appointed, in addition to *Mahāpurohita*, evidently to look after the Department of Religion. Both *Mahāpurohita* and *Dharmapradhāna* are found simultaneously mentioned in the Jabalpur Plates of Jayasiṁha of (K) E. 918[37] and Kumbhi Plates of Vijayasiṁha of (K) E. 931.[38] This indicates the waning influence of the *Mahāpurohita* as an important functionary of the State. His influence came to an end during the regime of the Kalachuris of Ratanpur, none of whose records refer *Mahāpurohita*. Mention is made in the Kharod Stone Inscription of Ratnadeva III[39] of another officer called *Dharmakarmādhikārin* who was probably synonymous with *Dharmapradhāna*.

*Mahāpurohita* as a State Official during the Paramāra regime is mentioned in the *Tilakamañjarī* of Dhanapāla.

**Mahādharmādhikaraṇika**

He was probably the head of the judicial department, *i.e.* the Chief Justice. The Dhureti Plates of Trailokyamalla mentions a *Pañcakula Dharmādhikaraṇa*[40] which was probably a court managed by a *Pañcakula*. If such *Dharmādhikaraṇas* (courts) were managed by the Kalachuris, the *Mahādharmādhikaraṇika* seems to be the head of such courts (*i.e.* the Chief Jistice) and not the Head of the Department of Religion as supposed by Dr. Mirashi.[41] Dr. Kane also points out *Dharmādhikaraṇa* as court of justice (vide *Śukra* IV. 5.44) or *Dharmādhikaraṇin* as judge (Vide *Matsyapurāṇa* 215.24).[42] Monier Williams also mentions *Dharmādhikaraṇika* as a judge or an administrator of law. The officer is found mentioned in the Banaras Plates of Karṇa of (K) E. 793[43] and Goharwa Plates of Karṇa.[44] He was the final appellate authority for cases coming from the lower courts, except when the king decided them himself.

**Mahāsaṁdhivigrahika**

He was the Minister for Peace and War and must have occupied an important place in the Kalachuri administration throughout their reign. The Kalachuris were occupied with a series of defensive as well as offensive wars. This minister figures several times in the Kalachuri inscriptions[45], sometimes simply designated as *Sāndhivigrahika*.[46] The records of the early Kalachuris[47] state that *Mahāsāndhivigrahādhikaraṇādhikṛta*, which is another term for the same officer, drafted the copper plate charters. This practice seems to have continued by the later Kalachuris also, though there is no specific mention of it. One expects revenue minister to draft such charters but the work was usually entrusted to the minister for peace and war probably because the charters had to describe the genealogy and the exploits of the grantor and his family and this minister had the most reliable and up-to-date information on this point. In this respect, there is agreement between the epigraphical practice and the dicta of the contemporary *smṛtis*. An anonymous text quoted in the *Mitākṣara* on Yājñavalkya states that 'the drafter (of copper plate charters) should be the person who is foreign minister; he should draft the charter as dictated by the king himself.[48]

Reference to this official of the Paramāras of Malwa also occurs in their records (vide, *JASB*, V, p.378). A casual mention of *Sāndhivigrahika* is found in the Dhureti Copper Plate of the Candellas (vide *EI*, XXV, pp.1 ff) also.

**Mahāsenāpati**

He was the highest military officer of the State, the Commander-in-chief of the king's army. Inscriptions of the early Kalachuris designate this officer as *Mahābalādhikṛta.*[49] Curiously enough, neither the inscriptions of the Tripuri branch nor that of Ratanpur branch refer to this officer. Only the Kahla Plates of Soḍhadeva, of the Sarayūpāra branch of the Kalachuris, mention this officer.[50] Inscriptions of the Tripuri and the Ratanpur branches simply refer to *Mahāśvasādhanika* and *Mahāpramattavāra* who were lower in rank than the Commander-in-chief. This is probably because the king himself was the Commander-in-chief of the army and worked with the heads of the four constituents of his four fold army.

**Mahāśvasādhanika**

He was the 'Great Equerry', *i.e.* the Commander-in-chief of the cavalry force. The *Arthaśāstra* of Kauṭilya which refers in detail to the duties of this officer designates him as *Aśvādhyakṣa.*[51] This officer is referred to in a number of Kalachuri inscriptions.[52] In the Jabalpur Plates of Jayasiṁha of (K)E. 918[53] he is simply mentioned as *Aśvasādhanika.* The Kumbhi Plates of Vijayasiṁha[54] mentions this officer as *Aśvasādhanaka,* which is the same as *Aśvasādhanaka.*

**Mahāpramattavāra**

He was the Chief Commander of the elephant force. In the inscriptions of the early Kalachuris, he is called *Mahāpīlupati.*[55] The Sankheda Plates of Śaṅkaragaṇa state[56] that *Mahāpīlupati* Nihirullaka was also *Bhogikapālaka* (*i.e.* head of a territorial division) and he had his own *Balādhikṛta* (military officer) named Śāntilla and also other officers. This indicates the influential position enjoyed by him. Later Kalachuri inscriptions designate this officer as *Mahāpramattavāra* and reference to this officer is found in Goharwa Plates of Karṇa.[57] The Jabalpur Plates of Jayasiṁha mention him simply as *Pramattavār*[58] whereas the Kumbhi Plates of Vijayasiṁha refers to this officer as *Pravātvavāra*.[59]

**Mahāsādhanika**

He was probably military officer, lower in rank than the Commander-in-chief of the army, probably in charge of military supplies. Reference to this officer is found in the Kahla Plates of Sodhadeva (V) E. 1135.[60]

**Mahāsāmanta or Mahāsāmantādhipati**

He was the great chieftain, the chief of feudatory. In the Kalachuri empire, as in the earlier ones, there were a number of feudal chieftains who owed allegiance to the emperor and most probably *Mahāsāmanta* was the minister-in-charge of the department dealing with the feudal vassals A number of Kalachuri inscriptions refer to this officer.[61] The Bahuribandh Stone Inscription of Gayākarṇa designates him as *Mahāsāmantādhipati*.[62]

**Mahāpramātṛ**

He was probably the Chief Revenue Officer or the Chief Surveyor, the head of the Revenue department. A number of Kalachuri inscriptions refer to this officer.[63] According to Dr. Kane, however, *Pramātṛ* in ancient India, was probably a Civil Judge.[64]

**Mahābhāṇḍagārika**

This officer corresponds to modem Chancellor of Exchequer — the Chief Keeper of the royal treasury. A large part of the Government revenue in this period was collected in kind and so this title given to the minister-in-charge of treasury is significant. *Bhāṇḍāgāra*, in this sense, has been used by Merutuṅga[65] and the Basārh seal of Chandragupta II.[66] In the *Arthaśāstra* of Kauṭilya, this officer is called *Sannidhātṛ*.[67] The officer is referred to in a number of Kalachuri inscriptions.[68] In the Jabalpur Plates of Jayasiṁha of (K) E. 918[69] and the Kumbhi Plates of Vijayasiṁha of (K) E. 932,[70] he is simply referred to as *Bahāṇḍāgārika*.

**Mahākṣapaṭalika**

'*Akṣapaṭala*' means 'Accounts Officer' (Stein) or 'Record office' (Fleet) so that *Mahākṣapaṭalika* was the Chief Keeper of Records or Accounts. In our grants we no doubt find king making grants and the foreign minister usually drafting them. But the officer who must have been principally consulted by the king must obviously have been *Mahākṣapaṭalika* whose office used to keep the necessary records connected with the land tenures and ownership. Reference to this officer occurs in a number of Kalachuri inscriptions.[71]

**Mahākaraṇika and Arthalekhin**

*Karṇika* in Ancient India was officer-in-charge of a ṣtate department so that the *Mahākaraṇika* seems to be the head of the Secretariat, *i.e.* the Chief Secretary. The officer is found mentioned in the Banaras Plates of Karṇa of (K) E. 793.[72] According to Dr. Mirashi, the title

*Arthalekhin* probably also corresponded to the 'Chief Secretary'.[73] The officer is mentioned in a number of Kalachuri inscriptions.[74]

**Mahādhyakṣa**

He was the Great Superintendent who probably exercised supervision over all departments. He is referred to in the Banaras Plates of Karṇa[75] and the Khairha Plates of Yaśaḥkarṇa.[76]

**Mahāpratihāra**

He was the Chief Usherer — the Great Chamberlain, the Superior officer above all door-keepers, attendants etc. It was his duty to arrange ushering of people into the royal presence. Reference to this officer is found in a number of Kalachuri inscriptions[77] as well as records of the Paramāras of Malwa.

**Mahāmahattaka**

This official is mentioned as *Mahāmahantaka* in the Kahla Plates of Soḍhadeva of (V) E. 1135.[78] The nature of his duties etc. cannot be ascertained in absence of sufficient data. *Mahāmahattaka* appears as title of king Gāṅgeyadeva in his Makundpur Stone Inscription of (K) E. 772,[79] and of feudatory Malayasiṃha in the Dhureti Plates of Trailokyamalla of (K) E. 963.[80]

**Mahāśreṣṭhi**

He was the Chief Banker. The officer is found mentioned in the Kahla Plates of Soḍhadeva.[81] The Amoda Plates of Pṛthvīdeva I mentions a *Śreṣṭhi* (banker) named Yaśa[82] who is referred to as the Mayor of Ratanpur in the Ratanpur Stone Inscription of Jājalladeva I of (K) E. 866.[83]

**Mahāpañcakulika**

He was the Chief of the *Pañcakulas*. The *Pañcakula*, was a committee of persons elected by the residents of a town or a village for the management of several departments. The officer is found mentioned in the Kahla Plates of Soḍhadeva of (V) E. 1135.[84]

**Dūtaka**

The inscriptions of the early Kalachuris mention *Dūtaka* as a higher officer whose duty was to convey king's command about the grant of land to local officers. The officer is invariably referred as military officer; in one instance, a Commander of Elephants (*mahāpīlupati*),[85] in two other instances the Commander-in-chief of the army (*mahābalādhikṛta*).[86] No reference to this officer is found in the inscriptions of the later Kalachuris. The official is also referred to in the inscriptions of the Paramāras of Malwa (Vide, *EI*, IX, p. 120).

Of the various lists of officials supplied by the different inscriptions of the Kalachuris, if we take the list of the Jabalpur Plates of Jayasiṁha and Kumbhi Plates of Vijayasiṁha[87] and compare them with the lists of other records referred to above, we find that the titles of a great number of officers in the former two records are stripped of the prefix of '*Mahā*'. Whether this addition is merely ornamental or to be taken as signifying a distinctive status superior to that of others who have been given such designation without the prefix, is a matter of conjecture. Possibly, it points to the tendency in the administrative system towards greater organisation, further concentration of power and unity of control which manifested itself in the appointment of heads even among some of the highest ranks of officials.

Records of the Paramāras of Malwa and the Candellas of Jejākabhukti supply list of some more high officials of the state. These are:

**Mahādaṇḍanāyaka and Daṇḍanāyaka**

He seems to be a military officer entrusted with other duties also. The *Tilakamañjarī* speaks of *Daṇḍanāyaka* for north India as well as *Dakṣiṇāpatha.*[88] Srī Chandra was *Daṇḍanāyaka* incharge of the region around Bhilsa.[89]

**Tantrapāla**

He seems to be an officer of the borders and his duty was to look after the interest the state. The Maser inscription of *Śulki* chief refers to one *Tantrapāla* of Paramāra ruler Muñja of Malwa.[90]

**Dharmastheya and Others**

*Dharmastheya* (Judicial Officer),[91] *Akṣapaṭalika* (keeper of accounts),[92] *Lekhakārika* (carrier of Kings correspondence),[93] *Kośakarakṣaka* (keeper of royal treasury), *Mahāvaidya* (the chief physician),[94] *Aṅgarakṣaka*[95] (incharge of body-guards of the king), *Sayyāpālaka* (incharge of beds of the king).[96] *Vandiputra* (the royal bard),[97] *Narmasaciva* (entertainer of the king),[98] *Aṁtarvaṁśika* (incharge of royal seragolia)[99] are some of the officers of the Central government referred to in the records of the Paramāras of Malwa.

Some interesting terms of high officaial found in the inscriptions of the Candellas are *Kośādhikarādhipati* (incharge of treasury establishment),[100] *Dharmalekhī* and *Arthalekhī* (writer of legal documents)[101], *Senāpati* (commander in chief of army)[102], *Koṭṭapāla* and *Ekāśvagoptā* (military officials).

## REFERENCES

1. *CII.* IV. Ins. no. 45 verses 30-37.
2. *Ibid.*, Ins. no. 60 verses 17-22.
3. *Ibid.*, Ins. no. 42 verse 32.
4. *Ibid.*, Appdx. 4 verse 27.
5. *Ibid.*, Ins. no. 95 verse 30.
6. *Ibid.*, Ins. no. 14 line 33.
7. *Ibid.*, Ins. no. 45 line 18.
8. *Ibid.*, Ins. no. 69 line 1.
9. *Ibid.*, Ins. no. 77 verse 22.
10. *Śurkranīti,* II, line 23.
11. *CII,* IV. Ins. nos. 76 lines 8-9; 77 lines 5-6 etc.
12. *Ibid.*, no. 64 verse 40.
13. *Ibid.*, verse 39.
14. *Ibid.*, Ins. nos. 63, 70, and Appdx. 4.
15. *Ibid.*, Ins. no. 64 verses 5-34:
16. *Ibid.*, Ins. no. 70.
17. *JASB,* XXXI, pp. 123 ff.
18. *CII.* IV. Ins. no. 42 verse 6.
19. *Ibid.*, Ins. no. 106 verse 13.
20. *Ibid.*, Ins. no. 42, 48, 50, 56, 57, 70, 76, 77, 84, 105 etc.
21. *Ibid.*, Ins. 42 verse 7.
22. *Ibid.*, no. 70 line 9.
23. *JASB,* XXXI, Ins. no. 100 verse 26.
24. *CII* IV., Ins. no. 56 verse 8.

25. *Ibid.*, Ins. nos. 107 verse 9; 116, line 4 & 117 line 4.
26. *Ibid.*, Ins. no. 90 verses 22-33.
27. *CII*, IV, pt. I, p. cxl.
28. *Śukra*, II, verse 82
29. *IA*, VI, p. 24.
30. *Ibid.*, VII, p. 304.
31. *CII*, IV Ins. no. 100 verses 25 and 27.
32. *Ibid.*, no. 90 verse 25.
33. *Ibid.*, no. 96 verse 11.
34. *Ibid.*, Ins. nos. 48, 50, 56, 57, 63, 100, 107, 111, 112, 116, 117, Appdx. 4 etc.
35. Compare the list of officers in Ins. nos. 63 and 70 with Appdx. 4 of *CII*, IV.
36. *CII*, IV. Ins. no. 56 verse 16
37. *Ibid.*, Ins. no. 63 line 22.
38. *Ibid.*, Appdx. 4 verse 27. Dr. Mirashi's view that *Mahāpurohita* was the same officer as *Dharmapradhāna* and that he was invariably the head of the religious department is difficult to accept in view of the evidence given above (vide *CII*, IV, pt. I, pp. cxxix, cxlii, clxvi).
39. *Ibid.*, Ins. no. 100 verse 44.
40. *Ibid.*, Ins. no. 72 line 9.
41. *Ibid.*, p. 249 fn. 8.
42. Kane, *History of Dharmaśāstra*, vol. III. pp. 343, 989.
43. *CII*, IV. Ins. no. 48 line 35.
44. *Ibid.*, Ins. no. 50, line 36.
45. *Ibid.*, Ins. nos. 48, 50, 74 and Appdx. 4.
46. *Ibid.*, Ins. no. 63, 70 and 77.
47. *Ibid.*, Ins. nos. 12, 14 and 15.
48. *Mitākṣarā* on *Yājñavalkya Smṛti*, Adhyāya I, v. 320; *EI*, XXI, p. 139.
49. *CII*, IV. Ins. no. 14 and 15
50. *Ibid.*, no. line 34.
51. *Arthaśāstra*, II. 30.

52. *CII*, IV, Ins. nos. 48, 50, 56, 57, Appdx. 2.
53. *Ibid.*, Ins. no. 63 line 24.
54. *Ibid.*, Appdx. 4 verse 27.
55. *Ibid.*, Ins. nos. 12 line 33 and 13 line 4.
56. *Ibid.*, Ins. no. 13 lines 4-5.
57. *Ibid.*, Ins. no. 50 lines 36-37.
58. *Ibid.*, Ins. no. 63 line 24.
59. *Ibid.*, Appdx. 4 verse 27.
60. *Ibid.*, Ins. no. 74 line 34.
61. *Ibid.*, Ins. nos. 48, 50, 56, 57, 63.
62. *Ibid.*, Ins. no. 59-c line 2.
63. *Ibid.*, Ins. nos. 48, 56, 57.
64. Kane, *History of Dharmaśāstra*, vol. III. p. 992.
65. *Prabandhaciñtāmaṇi*, Ed. by Jinavijayamuni, p. 53.
66. Raychaudhari, *Pol. Hist. of Ancient India*, p. 563.
67. *Arthaśāstra*, II. 4.
68. *CII*, IV. Ins. nos. 48, 50, 56, 57.
69. *Ibid.*, Ins. no. 63 line 24.
70. *Ibid.*, Appdx. 4, v. 27.
71. *Ibid.*, Ins. nos. 48, 50, 56, 57, 63, 74 and Appdx. 4.
72. *Ibid.*, no. 48 line 35.
73. *Ibid.*, p. 330 fn. 2.
74. *Ibid.*, Ins. nos. 63,70, Appdx. 4.
75. *Ibid.*, Ins. no. 48 line 30.
76. *Ibid.*, Ins. no. 56 line 26.
77. *Ibid.*, Ins. nos. 48, 50, 56, 57, 63, 70, 74 Appdx. 4; *Tilakamañjarī* of Dhanapāla, p. 58.
78. *Ibid.*, Ins. no. 74 line 34.
79. *Ibid.*, Ins. no. 47 line 1.
80. *Ibid.*, Ins. no. 72 line 8.
81. *Ibid.*, Ins. no. 74 line 34.
82. *Ibid.*, Ins. no. 76 verse 16.
83. *Ibid.*, Ins. no. 77 verse 12
84. *Ibid.* no. 74 line 34.

85. *Ibid.*, Ins. no. 12 line 33.
86. *Ibid.*, Ins. nos. 14 and 15.
87. *Ibid.*, Ins. no. 63 and Appdx. 4.
88. *Tilakamañjarī*, p. 66.
89. *CII*, VII, pp. 122-25.
90. *EI*, XIV, pp. 176-83
91. *Tilakamañjarī*, p.12.
92. *Ibid.*, p. 84. Also referred to in the Chakrahari plate of the Candellas.
93. *Ibid.*, p. 156.
94. *IHQ*, XXIII, p. 120. *Vaidya* in also mentioned in the Candella records.
95. *Tilakamañjarī*, p.12.
96. *Ibid.*, p. 156.
97. *Ibid.*, p. 12.
98. *Ibid.*
99. *Ibid.*, p. 59.
100. *EI*, I, p. 335, v. 6.
101. *EI*, IV, p. 170.
102. *IA*, XXV, p. 205.

## CHAPTER V

# DEPARTMENTS OF ADMINISTRATION

The Central Government in different parts of Central India, during the early medieval period, was ruled in uniform pattern. The departments of administration were uniform and so were the officers controlling them. The epigraphic and literary evidences provide the following evidence regarding the structure of the Central Government.

### The General Administration Department

This department with Prime Minister as its head resembled the *Śrī Karaṇa* (chief secretariat) of the Cāḷukyas.[1] The duties of officer like *Mahākaraṇika* and *Arthalekhin* (chief secretary) and *Mahādhyakṣa* (supervisor of all the department) seem to have allied with his department.

### The Department of Royal House-hold

The tradition of keeping the palace and its precincts safe, was enjoined by ancient Indian authorities like Śukra[2] and it was put into practice by the Paramāras, the Candellas and similarly by the Kalachuris. The ingress into and the egress from palace and the royal camp, were controlled by *dvārapālas* whose chief was *Mahāpratihāra* referred to in the inscriptions of all the above mentioned three dynasties. The management of the harem is referred in the Kalachuri inscriptions to have been entrusted to a Superintendent of the harem (*antarvaṁśika*).[3] *Sārikā*, courtezans and maid-servants, connected with the royal harem, are also referred to in Kalachuri inscriptions.[4] *Bālarāmāyaṇa* of Rājaśekhara also refers to the officers of the harem.[5] *Kañcukī*, the Chamberlain is mentioned in Candella inscriptions. *Śayyāpālaka* referred to in Paramāra inscriptions was perhaps guard of the bed of the ruler.[6]

**The Department of Foreign Affairs**

This department, which in ancient times was called *Sandhi-Vigraha Adhikaraṇa* (department of peace and war) was headed by *Mahāsāndhivigrahika*. If this department dealt with the feudatories also, as was usually the case in ancient India, the duties of *Mahāsāmantādhipati* was also allied with it. Further, as *Mahāsāndhivigrahika* was also responsible for writing the royal orders, he was assisted by a number of officers like *Lekhanādhyakṣa*,[7] *Ādeśanaibandhika*,[8] *Karaṇika*,[9] *Sūtradhāra*,[10] *Dharmalekhin*,[11] and *Daśamulin* etc.[12]

**Military and Police Department**

The military department was headed by the king or the *Mahāsanāpati* who were assisted by *Mahāśvasādhanika* (in-charge of the cavalry), *Mahāpramattavāra* (in charge of elephant force), *Koṭṭapāla* (?) (incharge of forts), and *Mahāsādhanika* (in charge of military supplies). *Balādhikṛta*,

*Aśvasādhanika* and *Pramattavāra* were probably officers next in rank. Gaulmika[13] was a subordinate officer who, according to *Śukranīti*[14] headed thirty foot soldiers. *Balādhira, Nāyaka, Chāṭa* and *Bhāṭa* were some more subordinate officers, the nature and functions of whose duties have been discussed below.[15]

The Police Department had a Superintendent of criminals called *Duṣṭasādhya.*[16] At the village level, this department had a number of officials, details about which are discussed below.[17]

The departments of military and police were helped by spies, the Superintendent of which is called *Charādhyakṣa* in the Kumbhi Plates of Kalachuri Vijayasiṁha.[18] Importance of spies is emphasised upon by Rājaśekhara in his *Bālarāmāyaṇa* thus: "Government which abounds in diplomatic devices, is not possible for those who do not employ secret state emissaries. Goddess of fortune, whom it is not easy to propitiate causes a sovereign to fall from his place when he is unwary."[19] Rājaśekhara further refers to the rules and methods to be followed by the spies for extracting information from the people.

**Revenue Department**

This department which was responsible for collection of revenue in cash and kind was headed by *Mahāpramātṛ.* The officer-in-charge called *Mahākṣapaṭalika,* who kept an accurate record of fields and boundaries, must have been working in close collaboration with this department, though not necessarily under it. The machinery of this department operated through a number of officers at the towns and villages.

**Treasury Department**

With the closure of the work of the Revenue department commenced the duties of the Treasury department. In ancient times, for the Treasury, it was not merely the question of striking balance and keeping the bullion safe in custody. The state revenue in those times was collected in cash and kind and careful steps had to be taken to keep them safe and fresh. The head of the department is designated in the Kalachuri inscriptions as *Mahābhāṇḍāgārika* or simply *Bhāṇḍāgārika.*

**The Department of Records**

The successful working of the above two departments depended much on the working of the Department of Records which was headed by an Inspector General of Records, called in the Kalachuri inscriptions as *Mahākṣapaṭalika* or simply *Akṣapaṭalika.* He was assisted by the Keeper of Records (*rakṣapaṭala*).[20]

**The Department of Religion**

This department, with *Mahāpurohita, Dharmapradhāna* or *Dharmakarmādhikārin* as its head was responsible for looking after the religion of the country. Another officer named *Mahāsādhanika* arranged for the *Mahādānas* (great gifts) of the King.

**The Department of Justice**

King being the fountain-source of justice, was expected to be the head of this department. But he was represented by the Chief Justice, called in the Kalachuri inscriptions *Mahādharmādhikaraṇika.* The *Pañcakula Dharmādhikaraṇas* which were village-courts, were managed by the pañcāyats which acted at the village level.

In case of the Paramāras of Malwa, we hear of *Dharmastheya* in *Tilakmañjarī.*[21] The Department of *Dharma* is mentioned as *Dharmādhikara* in the Khajuraho record of Candella King Dhaṅga, dated V.S. 1059.

## REFERENCES

1. *Śrī-Karaṇa* according to A.K. Majumdar (vide his '*Chalukyas of Gujarat*', p. 212), is the Chief Secretariat, whereas according to Dr. Mirashi, it is Record office (vide *CII*, IV, p. 544).
2. *Śukra*, II. 119.
3. *Ibid.*, Ins. no. 42 verse I. 4. Also *Tilakamañjarī*, p. 59.
4. *Ibid.*
5. *Bālarāmāyaṇa*, Act I, *śloka* 42.
6. *Tilakamañjarī*, p. 156.
7. *CII*, IV, Ins. no. 113 line 1.
8. *Ibid.*, Ins. no; 74 line 57.
9. *Ibid.*, Ins. no. 45 verse 36.
10. *Ibid.*, Ins. no. 44, 45 etc.
11. *Ibid.*, Ins. no. 56 line 44; *EI*, IV, p 170.
12. *Ibid.*, Ins. no. 63 line 40.
13. *Ibid.*, Ins. no. 74 l. 34. Dr. Kane is of opinion (that *Gaulimka* was Supdt. of Woods and Forests (*History of Dharmaśāstra*, p. 982). In view of Śukra's, authority quoted, the view mentioned above seems to be more plausible.
14. *Śukranīti*, ch. II, v. 117-18.
15. See below: Village Administration.
16. *CII*, IV, Appdx. 4 v. 27.
17. See below, under, Village Administration.

18. *CII,* IV, Appdx. 4 v. 27.
19. *Bālarāmāyaṇa,* Act I, śloka 24.
20. *CII.* IV, Ins. no. 96 verse 40.
21. *Tilakamañjarī,* p. 12.

# CHAPTER VI

# THE TERRITORY *(RĀṢṬRA)*

## The Administrative Units

The terms used for various administrative divisions in different parts of Central India during the early medieval period differed from branches to branches of the dynasties ruling over the regions. There were many terms which were used in common. In some cases the terms have been used confusingly. In other cases deeper investigation is still necessary to understand the significance of the terms.

As far as the kingdom of the Paramāras of Malwa is concerned, the entire territory was known as *Mālavadeśa.* For the purpose of administration, the empire was divided into a number of *Maṇḍalas, i.e.* Provinces which were governed by Governors. We find names of Seventeen Provinces of the Paramāra empire in their inscriptions.[1]

The *Maṇḍalas* were further divided into *Viṣaya, Bhoga, Pathaka* and *Pratijāgaraṇaka* which are equivalents of modern districts. We find names of number of districts in the inscriptions of the Paramāras of Malwa.[2]

The *Grāma* or the village was the lowest unit in the administrative set up of the Paramāras of Malwa. A large number of village names occur in their records.[3] The names of the villages usually ended with term like *padra, padraka, grāma* etc. The village granted to the Brāhmaṇas was known as *agrahāra* and the village inhabitated by the Brāhmaṇas was known as *brahmasthāna* on *Brahmapuri*. The prefix *śrī* was often added to the capital towns.[4] The names of the towns ended with *pura, purī, nagara,* and *nagari*.

As for the Candellas, on the evidence of inscriptions, the territorial divisions may be defined as follows:

The state as a whole was known as Jejakābhukti which for the administrative reasons was divided into a number of districts, sub-divisions and village groups. The village (*grāma*) was the limit of administration, some villages were grouped together to form unions. Thus there were village groups comprising of 5, 12, or 18 villages. Numbers of them are referred to in the inscriptions of the Candellas.[5] The next territorial unit was *pattalā*, denoting a unit larger than a village. We come across names of large number of *pattalās* in the inscriptions of the Candellas.[6] Sometimes *pattalā* and *viṣaya* are used in idential sense. The next larger unit was *avasthā* or Sub-Division reference to which occurs number of times.[7] Another expression which seems to be almost synonymous is *pratibaddham*. The term *viṣaya* signified the next higher unit of administration and names of a number of them occur in the inscriptions of the dynasty.[8] Sometimes *maṇḍala* and *viṣaya* are used denoting the same sense. The term *bhukti* is not known to have been used by the Candellas in the sense of an administrative unit larger than a *viṣaya*. Their kingdom itself was known as Jejākabhukti. Villages granted to the Brāhmaṇas are mentioned as *bhaṭṭāgrahara*. References to some cities and towns (*nagaras*) and places important for royal encampments also occur in the Candella records.[9]

A better picture is provided by the inscriptions of various branches of the Kalachuri dynasty. A study of the inscriptions of the early Kalachuris shows that the terms for the territorial divisions used therein, are *viṣaya, bhoga, rāṣṭra,* and *grāma*. The *grāma* was undoubtedly the smallest territorial division as it had always been. Relation between *viṣaya, bhoga* and *rāṣṭra,* however, seems to be problematic. While the Sarsavni Plates of Buddharāja of (K)E. 361,[10] refer to village Kumarīvaḍao situated in the Gorajjā *bhoga* which was included in the Bharukachchha *viṣaya,* pointing thereby that *bhoga* was smaller unit than *viṣaya,* the same inscription along with the Vadner Plates of Buddharāja of (K)E. 360.[11] and Abhona Plates of Śaṅkaragaṇa of (K)E. 347,[12] mention *viṣyapati* (head of a *viṣaya*) next to *bhogika* (head of the *bhoga*) in the chronological list of officers to whom the grant is addressed. That *viṣaya* was not necessarily larger than *bhoga* is further confirmed by the reference in the Abhona plates of Śaṅkaragaṇa to the village Vallisikā situated in the *viṣaya* of Bhogavardhana.[13] Regarding the significance of the term *rāṣṭra,* occuring in the Abhona Plates of Śaṅkaragaṇa[14] and Vadner and Sanasavni Plates of Buddharāja,[15] views of scholars are not satisfactory. While Dr. Altekar is of opinion[16] that under the early Kalachuris, was larger than *rāṣṭra* and Dr. V.V. Mirashi seems to support him,[17] Dr. Gupta translates the term *rāṣṭra* as a province.[18] The problem needs deeper investigation. The inscription of the later Kalachuris point to the use of changed terminology.

The inscriptions of the Kalachuris of Tripuri mention the term *viṣaya* representing a district. The *viṣaya* referred to in the inscriptions are those of Kakanda-Kuṭu,[19] Navapattalā,[20] and Samudrapāṭa.[21] Probably, the term *uddeśa* [22] also represented a district.

The next territorial division representing a modern tehsil was designated as *pattalā*. It is interesting to note that of all the records of the various branches of the Kalachuris, it is only the inscriptions of the Tripuri branch which record this term representing a tehsil. The *pattalās* referred to in the inscriptions of the Kalachuris are those of Devagrāma[23] Jāulī,[24] Khandagahā,[25] Kūyīsambāpalisa,[26] Rewa,[27] Dhanavāhī,[28] Sambalā,[29] Nava[30] and Kauśāmba.[31]

A third term which the inscriptions of the Tripuri branch use rather confusingly is *maṇḍala*. This term occurs only twice in their inscriptions. The Bheraghat Stone Inscription of Narasiṁha of (K)E. 907, which refers to *Mālavamaṇḍala*, uses the term *maṇḍala* in the sense of a Country.[32] The Karitalai Stone Inscription of Lakṣmaṇarāja II, which refers to the "whole of *maṇḍala* which gave the alms at four thrashing floors", refers to the term *maṇḍala* in a much narrower sense of representing a smaller territorial unit.[33] Further, in the title of *Mahāmaṇḍaleśvara* often referred to in the inscriptions, the term *maṇḍala* stands for a province. The use of the term *maṇḍala* in the inscriptions of the Kalachuris of Tripuri is, thus, much confusing. It is noteworthy that in later times, this term was specifically used by the Kalachuris of Ratanpur to represent a modern tehsil.

Sometimes, the inscriptions of the Kalachuris of Tripuri refer to the terms *bhūmi* and *āhāra* to represent a sub-division. Thus, the Karitalai Stone Inscription of

Lakṣmaṇarāja II mentions the *āhāra* of Dhavalā in which the village Challi pāṭaka was situated.[34] Similarly, the Banaras Plates of Karṇa of (K)E. 793 refer to the *bhūmi* of Kāśī in which the village Srusī was situated.[35]

The *pattalās* included cities, termed as *pura,*[36] *purī,*[37] *pattana,*[38] and *nagara,*[39] etc. and villages (*grāma*). The capital cities were called *Rājadhāni.*[40] The villages were sometimes grouped together to form a territorial unit. Thus, the Karitalai Stone Inscription of Lakṣ̄amaṇarāja II mentions the Mālā group of twelve villages in which the donated village Vaṭagartikā was situated.[41] Habitation at a particular locality was, sometimes, termed as *nikāya.*[42]

The above mentioned terms used by the Kalachuris of Tripuri were changed during the regime of the Kalachuris of Ratanpur. The terms used for the largest territorial unit representing a Country is *Janapada.* Thus, the Ratanpur Stone Inscription of Jājalladeva I of (K)E. 866, refers to the *Janapada* of Dakṣiṇakośala whose capital was at Tummāṇa.[43] Next to the country, representing a province is the term *deśa.* The inscription of the Ratanpur branch refers to the desas of Bhattavila,[44] Vihарā,[45] Kākayara,[46] Tamanāla,[47] Bhramaravadra[48] and Tummāṇa.[49] Sometimes the term *deśa* is used synonymous with *maṇḍala* which at that time represented a much smaller unit. Thus, the Amoda Plates of Pṛthvīdeva I refer to Madhyadeśa which, in fact, refers to *Madhya maṇḍala*[50] (the territory round modern Bilaspur in M.P.).

The term *viṣaya,* representing the next territorial unit *viz.* a District, was continued to be used by the Ratanpur branch of the Kalachuris as well as by the Tripuri branch. The Sheorinarayan Plates of Ratnadeva II of (K)E. 878, refer to Anarghavallī *viṣaya* in which the village Tiṇeri[51] was situated. Similarly, the Tahankapar Plates of Pamparājadeva refer to an un-named *viśaya*.[52]

Between the District and the village stood the *maṇḍala*, representing modern tehsil. The term *maṇḍala*, used by the administration of the Ratanpur branch of the Kalachuris and their successors, was a substitute for the term *pattalā* of the Tripuri branch of the Kalachuris. The *maṇḍala* referred to in inscriptions are those of Komo,[53] Apara,[54] Sāgatta,[55] (or Sāmanta), Khimiḍī,[56] Vairāgarh,[57] Lañjikā,[58] Bhāṇāra,[59] Talahāri,[60] Daṇḍakapura,[61] Nanāvalī,[62] Kukkuṭa,[63] Anarghavallī,[64] Evaḍi,[65] Madhya[66] and Dakṣiṇakośala.[67] Sometimes the term *maṇḍala* is used in much wider sense of country (*deśa*). Thus, the Ratanpur Stone Inscription of Pṛthvīdeva II of (V) E. 1207,[68] refers to the *Cedi-maṇḍala* which, in fact, stands for the Cedi country. Similarly, the Ratanpur Stone Inscription of Jājalladeva I refers to the Āndhra *maṇḍala*, which, in fact, stands for Āndhradeśa. Also, we have seen above how Madhyadeśa is used synonymous with Madhya *maṇḍala*. The term *maṇḍala* is again sometimes, used in the sense of a province. This can be inferred from the title of *Mahāmaṇḍaleśvara* referred to in a number of inscriptions used by the Governors of the provinces. The statements of the Amoda Plates of Pṛthvīdeva I[69] and of Ratanpur Stone Inscription of Jājalladeva I,[70] that the eighteen sons of Kokalla I were made "the lords of the *maṇḍalas*" also, imply that the term *maṇḍala* has been used in the sense of a province. The term *maṇḍala* was again sometimes used synonymous with the term *bhūmi*. Thus, the Rajim Stone Inscription of Pṛthvīdeva II of K.E. 896,[71] refers to the *bhūmi* of Talahāri, meaning actually, the Talalahāri-*maṇḍala*. At other times, the term was used synonymous with *bhukti* or *bhoga*. Thus, the *maṇḍala* of Daṇḍakapura of the Ratanpur Stone Inscription of Jājalladeva I[72] called Daṇḍabukti in the Koni Stone Inscription of Pṛthvīdeva II of (K)E 900.[73] *Bhukti* was synonymous with *bhoga*, the in-charge of which is called *Bhogina* in the Ratanpur Stone Inscription of Pṛthvīdeva II of (K)E. 915.[74]

The *maṇḍalas* consisted of towns (*pura* or *pattana*), capitals (*rājadhānī*) and villages (*grāma*).[75] We come across another term *viz. paṭṭikā* in the Sheorinarayan Inscription of Jājalladeva II of (K)E. 919.[76] Verse 13 of the inscription states that Someśvara obtained Soṇṭhiva-*paṭṭikā* as part of his heritage. Again, verse 35 of the same inscription states that at Soṇṭhivapura, Sarvadeva made a temple of Śiva to be constructed. It seems that Soṇṭhiva-*paṭṭikā* stood for the region surrounding Soṇṭhivapura. That *pattikā* stood for a territorial division is also indicated in the Tahankapar plates of Pamparājadeva II of (K)E. 905[77] and the Kalachhala plates of Īśvarāta.[78] The latter mentions that the village Kupikā was situated in the *paṭṭa* (territorial division) of Vankika. It is noteworthy that the term *paṭṭa* was an ancient one, which was used for *kupikā* also. The Khoh Copper Plates of Mahārāja Hastin refer to the Agrahāra of Koparika in the northern *paṭṭa*.[79]

The inscriptions of the Sarayūpāra branch of the Kalachuris refer to the term *viṣaya*,[80] *grāma*, *kṣetra*[81] (within a village) and an unnamed sub-division.[82] No other technical term representing a territorial division is available in the inscriptions of the *Sarayūpāra* branch of the Kalachuris.

**Provincial Administration**

In case of the Malwa region where the Paramāras ruled, the kingdom was divided into number of provisions (*maṇḍalas*) which were ruled by the Governors who were of two types, *viz.*, the ordinary Governors and the feudatory chiefs. The feudatories though deprived of their independence retained some of their lands. The feudatory princes were known by the generic title *Māṇḍalikas*, but sometimes they styled themselves as *Mahāmaṇḍaleśvara, Maṇḍaleśvara, Narendra, Nṛpa, Mahākumāra, Mahāsāmanta, Sāmanta, Rājaputra* and *Ṭhakkura*. The Parāmara court was full of feudatory chiefs and they took their seats in the royal court according to their grades. A study of the Paramāra inscriptions and contemporary literature shows that at provincial level of administration there were four categories of feudatory chiefs.

The first category consisted of those offices who were rewarded by the king with land in consideration of their valuable services. Sometimes such officers were hereditary. To the second category belonged those chiefs who had not often built up their own principalities during the period of aggrandizement, though they acknowledged the supremacy of their overload. The third category comprised princes who had carved out their principalities in defiance of the central authority during the difficult days of the Paramāras. To the fourth category belonged those chiefs who were defeated and forced to accept the suzerainty of the Paramāras and were given the status of a vassal. According to A.S. Altekar,[83] the most important duties of the feudatories were to mention the name of the overlord; to attend the imperial court on ceremonial occasions, to pay regular tributes, to give presents on festive occasions and to send certain number of troops to the aid of the overlord in the event of emergency.

That the feudatories of the Paramāra rulers obeyed these conditions is evidenced by the contemporary inscriptions and literature. The measure of internal autonomy enjoyed by these lords varied according to circumstances. Under the Paramāra provincial administration, number of powerful feudatory chiefs came into existence and this tended to weaken the central authority.

Inscriptions of the Kalachuris also provide some information about provincial administration. At times the governors of provinces were members of royal family. We know how the eldest of the 18 sons of Kokalla I succeeded him to the Kalachuri throne of Tripuri and the younger ones were made "the lord of the *maṇḍalas.*"[84] Similarly, the Sheorinarayan Stone Inscription of Jājalladeva II of Cedi Era 919 states that Sarvadeva obtained Soṇṭhivapaṭṭikā as part of his heritage.[85] Sometimes the governorship of a province became hereditary in the family of a royal house so that in course of time they established their independent branch. It was in this way that the branches of Ratanpur and Raipur came into existence. When it was not possible to find suitable members of the royal family for the post of Governor, some capable officer of the government with considerable experience in administration was given governorship. Instances of Brahmadeva and Malayasiṁha are apparent in this respect. Such governors often enjoyed the status of feudatories and bore the titles of *Mahāsāmanta* or *Mahārānaka*, *Mandalika-agraṇī*, *Mahāmāṇḍalika*, *Mahāmaṇḍleśvara* and *Mahāsāmantādhipati*. The nature and status enjoyed by each of these feudatories do not appear to have been the same. Some of them enjoyed greater autonomy in their respective spheres and were entitled to have their courts at their capitals with all royal splendour *viz.* the use of throne, crown, banner etc., and above all, the *pañcamahāśabda*. To allow smooth administration sometimes powerful feudatories were allowed to have their own sub-feudatories. The smaller feudatories and the sub-feudatories enjoyed only less freedom and were under the control of their overlord. These Governor feudatories often maintained a separate army which they had to put at the disposal of their overlord when asked to do so. With their army they maintained peace and order and put down rebellions, if any. The governors, sometimes issued coins in their own names and this was a sign of their progress towards independence.

**District Administration**

The *Maṇḍalas* (provinces) during the reign of the Paramāras of Malwa, were further divided into *Viṣayas* and *Bhogas* which were equivalents of modern districts and sub-divisions of them. Contemporary inscriptions and literature do not provide the name of any officer in charge of a *Viṣayas* or *Bhoga*. He may have been *Viṣayapati* and *Bhogapati*.

Inscriptions of the Candellas supply names of a large number of *Viṣayas*.[86]

A better picture of the district administration is provided by the inscriptions of the the Kalachuris.

The *viṣaya* represented the district at all times in the Kalachuri administration. In the inscriptions of the early Kalachuris, the head of the *viṣaya* is called *Viṣayapati.*[87] That to these posts of *Viṣayapatis* were sometimes appointed important officers like ministers, is reflected in the Rewa Stone Inscription of Vijayasiṁha of (K.)E. 944 which records that Jāṭa, the illustrious minister of Karṇa was put in charge of a *viṣaya.*[88] These *Viṣayapatis* must have been responsible for maintaining law and order of the region of their control and for this, small military force might have been kept at their disposal, though we do not have any evidence of this in our inscriptions. The *Viṣayapatis* must have been exercising considerable revenue powers as they are invariably mentioned in the Copper Plates of the early Kalachuris where they are referred to among the officers ordered not to disturb the possession of the donees of lands or villages granted. An officer named *Viṣayadānika, i.e.* one who collected the revenue (*ādāna*) of the *Viṣaya,* is referred to in the Kahla Plates of Soḍhadeva.[89] He must have been working under the supervision of the *Viṣayapati.* That *Viṣayapatis* must have been responsible for keeping an accurate record of the ownership of land and grants made by the king is reflected in the Chhoti Deori Stone Inscription of Śaṅkaragaṇa I, which records that Chuṭunāgaka who was in charge of the *viṣaya* of Kakandakuṭu "himself recorded (the gift of) a granary in (the village of) Karikatin and Asekatin."[90] Nothing is known from the inscriptions of the Kalachuris regarding the control that the provinces exercised over the *viṣayas* or what the *viṣayas* exercised over the sub-divisions and villages.

**Sub-divisional Administration**

We have seen above that *viṣaya* (district) was divided into *bhoga* by the early Kalachuris, and into *maṇḍala, bhukti* or *bhoga* by the Kalachuris of the Ratanpur branch and their successors. In the Candella records the terms used for a sub division are *Avastha*[91] and *Pratibaddham.*[92] The terms for the officer-in-charge of the sub–division that we come across are : *bhogika* in the inscriptions of the early Kalachuris[93] and *bhogina*[94] in the inscriptions of the Kalachuris of Ratanpur. The term *Bhogikapālaka* which we come across in the Sankheda Plates of Śaṅkaragaṇa[95] stands for an officer who supervised the work of the *Bhogika.* As already observed above, an instance of this we come across in case of Mālā[96] (or Mālavaka) group[97] of twelve villages referred to in the Karitalai Stone Inscription of Lakṣmaṇarāja II. That Valleśvara, the donor gave as grant the village Vaṭagartikā (situated) in the Mālā group of twelve villages which was in his own territory (*svakīyaśāsane*) shows that individual officers were appointed on such groups of villages.

**Town Administration**

The cities and the towns were put in charge of Mayors. The Amoda Plates of Pṛthvīdeva I and Ratanpur Stone Inscription of Jājalladeva I refer to *śreṣṭhi* Yaśa who was Mayor of Ratnapura (*Ratnapura-pradhāna*).[98] Similarly, the Ratanpur Stone Inscription of Vāhara refers to Mayor Govinda who is called *Ratnapura prajādhīpa.*[99] About the powers enjoyed by Govinda, the record states that he "bears the burden of (governing) the kingdom of his lord and has power to do or desist from doing (anything)."[100] No further evidence regarding the administration of the cities is available in the Kalachuri inscriptions.

**Village Administration**

Village was the smallest territorial unit. In the inscriptions of the Kalachuris, the headman of the village is technically called *grāmaṇī*[101] or *paṭṭakila*[102] (corresponding to modern patel of villages). That he was a remunerated officer who used to receive his share by enjoying a tax called *paṭṭakiladāya* is referred to in the Jabalpur Plates of Vijayasiṁha of (K)E. 918 and his Kumbhi Plates of (K)E. 932.[103]

The actual process of the administration of a village is not known from the inscriptions. Duties of the following officers who are referred to in the inscriptions may give us a rough idea of the same.

1. *Śaulkika*[104] – He was the Superintendent of the tolls or customs duties.
2. *Tarapati*[105] – He was officer-in-charge of the ferries, responsible for their construction, development and up-keeping. He probably also collected the cess levied for their use.
3. *Ghaṭṭapati*[106] – He was officer-in-charge of the landing stations (*ghāṭa*). He was probably an officer different from *Ghaṭṭapāla* of the Panchobh Copper Plate of Saṅgramagupta,[107] who was a keeper of mountain passes.
4. *Duṣṭasādhya*[108] or *Duṣṭasādhaka*[109] – He was the village police officer, the mentor of criminals. In the Jabalpur Stone Inscription of Jayasiṁha we come across a tax

levied for *Dussādhyas* (*dussādhyadāya*).[110] Similarly, the Kumbhi Plates of Vijayasiṁha refer to tax levied for *duṣṭasādhakas* (*duṣṭasādhyadāya*).[111] It seems that the remunerations to police officers were paid out of this tax.

5. *Cāṭa* and *Bhāṭa*[112] – References to these two officers occur only in the inscriptions of the early Kalachuris and the Kalachuris of Sarayūpāra branch. These officers are invariably instructed in the records not to enter the *agrahāra* villages. The meaning of these two words in the charters of some of the dynasties of ancient India has given rise to various interpretations. According to Fleet, it means "regular and irregular soldiers."[113] Vogel, however, thinks that *Cāṭa* is equivalent to modem *car* or head of a *parganā* responsible for the internal management of a district for the collection of revenue and apprehension of criminals. He thinks that *Bhāṭa* which is usually compounded with *Cāṭa,* should be taken to mean "an official subordinate to the head of the *parganā.* [114] Bhagwanlal Indraji translates the term as "soldiers against robbers."[115] According to Prof. Pathak, *Chāṭas* are those that transgress the rules of conduct for decent people and *Bhāṭas* are servants telling falsehood.[116] Dr. Mirashi, Dr. Altekar, Dr. Sen and many other scholars support the view propounded by Fleet and the explanation seems to be most satisfactory. According to Dr. Mirashi, "the *Bhāṭas* and *Cāṭas* were forbidden to enter the *agrahāra* villages except when they had to apprehend thieves and persons accused of high treason. They were evidently royal servants whose duty it was to maintain peace and order in the

kingdom. They correspond to modern policemen and soldiers.[117] According to Dr. Altekar "*Cāṭas* and *Bhāṭas* were the members of the police and military forces of the State and when they were quartered in a village while on the march, the villagers had to meet a number of demands of their unwelcorned guests."[118] That was probably the reason why they were forbidden to enter the *agrahāra* villages. The invariable mention of *Bhāṭa* after *Cāṭa* probably hints to the subordinate status of the former.

6. *Nāyaka* – Kauṭilya mentions *Nāyaka* as one of the eighteen *mahāmātyas* important enough to be spied-upon.[119] According to *Śukranīti*, however, *Nāyaka* was the lord of ten villages[120] and most probably it is in this sense that the term has been used in the Tewar Stone Inscription of Jayasiṁha,[121] Raipur Stone Inscription of Brahmadeva[122] and the two Tahankapar Plates of Pamparājadeva.[123] If the Mālavaka of the Tewar Stone Inscription of Jayasiṁha is the same as the Mālā group of twelve villages (as shown above), most probably *Nāyaka* Keśava, whose place of residence was the village Sīkhā (in Mālavaka), was officer-in-charge of the Mālavaka. Quite possibly Nāyaka was a military officer who held lands from the king on military tenure, as in South Indian administrative system of *Nāyakara.*
7. *Balādhīra*[124] — He was probably a military officer, corresponding to *Balādhī* of the Cāḷukyạ administration[125] or *Balādhīpa* of the early Chauhan dynasties.[126]
8. *Mākutika* [127] – According to Dr. Mirashi "this may be a village officer corresponding to modern police patel

in Bombay State."[128]

9. *Khaṇḍavala*[129] – The term, as inscribed in the Kahla Plates of Soḍhadeva is a mistake for the term *Khaṇḍapāla* (the next term *Balādhīra* has actually been engraved *Valādhīra*) occurring in the Pāla grants, he was either a military officer[130] or an officer-in-charge of a comparatively small area (*khaṇḍa*).[131] The term *Khaṇḍapāla* occurring in the Panchob Copper Plates of Saṅgrāmagupta has been translated as "the Superintendent of municipal wards."[132]
10. *Gaintā* – The term occurring in the two Tahankapar Plates of Pamparājadeva belonging respectively to (K)E. 965[133] and 966[134] stands for the village priest. It is noteworthy that the term is still used in the same sense in the Bastar district from where the plates were discovered.
11. *Sāvu* – The term which appeared in the two copper plates of Pamparājadeva[135] probably stood for the term *Sāo,* the rich man of the village, who is called so even now in the region of the discovery of the plates.

**Village Council**

The above mentioned officers were guided in administration by the opinion of the village public, which made itself felt through the village elders, referred to as *mahattaras* in the inscriptions of the early Kalachuris and the Candellas.[136] In the Kahla Plate Soḍhadeva, we come across the term *mahattama.*[137] Since *mahattara* literally means "one higher in rank", and *mahattama* means "one highest in rank", the latter term implies an assembly of *mahattaras* in which the *mahattama* was the superior-most. The assembly of the *mahattaras* was known as *pañcakula,* the term which occurs in the Dhureti Plates of Candella Trailokyavarman.[138] Though the literal meaning of the term implies that the members of the Assembly must have been five, there is nothing in the inscriptions of the Kalachuris to indicate that it was so. Further, whether these members were elected or nominated is not known. Quite possibly, the procedure of election might have been followed as was usually the case in ancient India. The relation of the *pañcakula* with the Provincial and Central government is not known. The fact that the grants are-addressed to them, implies the supervising control of the central government over them. This is further evidenced by the presence of *Mahāpañcakulika* at the capital, reference to which occurs in the Kahla Plates of Soḍhadeva.[139] He must have been responsible for supervision over the *pañcakulas* of the country. About the nature of the duties, powers and functions of the *pañcakulas*, we have no reference in the Kalachuri inscriptions. They must have played an important part in defending the interests of the villagers and in promoting their material moral and intellectual progress. The reference in the Dhureti Plates of Trailokyamalla[140] about *pañcakuladharmādhikaraṇa* (a court of justice managed by *pañcakula*), implies that among other duties, the village assembly looked after the administration of justice at a particular locality.

## REFERENCES

1. For details, see. Bhatia, P., *The Paramaras*, p. 215. Also Jain, K.C., *Madhya Pradesh Through the Ages*, pp. 493 ff.
2. *Ibid.*

3. *Ibid.*
4. *IA*, XIX, p. 353.
5. See Mitra, S.K., *Early Rulers of Khajuraho*, Delhi, p.161. Also Bose, N.S., *History of the Candellas*, Calcutta, pp. 132-33.
6. *Ibid.*
7. *Ibid.*
8. *Ibid.*
9. *Ibid.*
10. CII. IV, Ins. no. 15, line 19.
11. *Ibid.*, Ins. no. 14, line 18.
12. *Ibid.*, Ins. no. 12, line 16-17.
13. *Ibid.*, line 18.
14. *Ibid.*, line 17.
15. *Ibid.*, Ins no. 14, line 18 & 15 line 18.
16. The *Rashtrakutas and their Times* (1934), p. 136.
17. Dr. Mirashi seems to contradict himself stating at one place that "some sub-divisions of *viṣaya* may have been known as *Rāṣṭras*" (p. cxxxv of *CII.* IV. pt. I) while at another place in the same context, he states that "*rāṣṭras* was a territorial division corresponding to modern Commissioner's Division" (p.43 n. 5 of *CII.* IV. pt. I).
18. *EI.* XII. p. 36.
19. CII. IV. Ins. no. 36 lines 6-7.
20. *Ibid.*, Ins. no. 64 verse 47.
21. *Ibid.*, Ins. no. 64 verse 4.
22. *Ibid.*, Ins. no. 56 lines 27-28.
23. *Ibid.*, Ins. no. 56 lines 27-28.
24. *Ibid.*, Ins. no. 60 verse 29 and Appdx. 2 v. 1.
25. *Ibid.*, Ins. no. 65 line 11.
26. *Ibid.*, Ins. no. 68 lines 7-8.
27. *Ibid.*, Ins. no. 70 line 30.
28. *Ibid.*, Ins. no. 72 line 10.
29. *Ibid.*; Appdx. 4 verse 27.

30. *Ibid.*, Ins. no. 64 line 26.
31. *Ibid.*, Ins. no. 50 line 7.
32. *Ibid.*, Ins. no. 60 verse 21.
33. *Ibid.*, Ins. no. 42 verse 42.
34. *CII.*IV, Ins. no. 42 verse 34.
35. *Ibid.*, Ins. no. 48 line 37.
36. *Ibid.*, Ins. nos. 42 verse 38; 56 verse 7 etc.
37. *Ibid.*, Ins. no. 88 line 17.
38. *Ibid.*, Ins. nos. 45 verse 19; 95 line 27.
39. *Ibid.*, Ins. no. 65 line 5.
40. *Ibid.*, Ins. no. 68 line 4.
41. *Ibid.*, Ins. no. 42 verse 36.
42. *Ibid.*, Ins. no. 62 line 5.
43. *Ibid.*, Ins. no. 77 verses 6-7.
44. *Ibid.*, Ins. no. 88 verse 3.
45. *Ibid.*, verse 4.
46. *Ibid.*, verse 17.
47. *Ibid.*, verse 13.
48. *Ibid.*, verse 16.
49. *Ibid.*, Ins. no. 93 verse 8.
50. *Ibid.*, Ins. no. 91 verses 15-16.
51. *Ibid.*, Ins. no. 82 line 19.
52. *Ibid.*, Ins. no. 117 line 9.
53. *CII.*IV. Ins. nos. 76 verse 12; 77 verse 13; 82 verse 5, 88 verse 6 etc.
54. *Ibid.*, Ins. no. 75 line 8.
55. *Ibid.*, Ins. no. 92 line 22.
56. *Ibid.*, verse 23.
57. *Ibid.*, Ins. nos. 90 verse 26 and 77 verse 23.
58. *Ibid.*, Ins. no. 77 verse 23.
59. *Ibid.*
60. *Ibid.*
61. *Ibid.*, Ins. nos. 77 verse 23; 90 verse 26; 96 verse 5; 88 verse 14.

62. *Ibid.*, Ins. no. 77 verse 23.
63. *Ibid.*
64. *Ibid.*, Ins. no. 83 verse 20.
65. *Ibid.*, Ins. no. 89 verse 16.
66. *Ibid.*, Ins. nos. 91 verses 15-16; 94 verse 15.
67. *Ibid.*, Ins. no. 77 verse 23.
68. *Ibid.*, Ins. no. 93 verse 8.
69. *Ibid.*, Ins. no. 76 verse 6.
70. *Ibid.*, Ins. no. 77 verse 5.
71. *Ibid.*, Ins. no. 88 verse 14.
72. *Ibid.*, Ins. no. 77 verse 23.
73. *Ibid.*, Ins. no. 90 verse 26.
74. *CII,* IV. Ins. no. 96 verse 13
75. *Ibid.*, Ins. no. 96 verse 36.
76. *Ibid.*, Ins. no. 98 verse 13
77. *Ibid.*, Ins. no. 116 line 8
78. *Ibid.*, Ins. no. 118 line 2.
79. *Ibid.*, IV. Ins. no. 22, p. 104.
80. *Ibid.*, IV. Ins. no. 73 verse 17
81. *Ibid.*, Ins. no. 74 line 36
82. *Ibid.*
83. Altekar, A.S, *State and Govt. in Ancient India,* p. 299.
84. *Ibid.*, Ins. no. 76 verse 6, 77 verse 5 etc.
85. *Ibid.*, Ins. no. 98 verse 13
86. See Mitra, S.K., *Early Rulers of Khajuraho* p. 163.
87. *CII,* IV, Ins. nos. 12 lines 16-17; 14 line 18; 15 line 18.
88. *Ibid.*, Ins. no. 7.
89. *Ibid.*, Ins. no. 74 line 35.
90. *Ibid.*, Ins. no. 36 lines 7-9.
91. Mitra, S.K., *op.cit.*, p.162.
92. *Ibid.*
93. *CII,* IV, Ins. nos. 12 line 17; 14 line 18; 15 line 17
94. *Ibid.*, Ins. nos. 96 verse 13 and footnote 1 of p. 509.
95. *Ibid.*, Ins. no. 13 line 4.

96. *Ibid.*, Ins. no. 42 verse 36.
97. *Ibid.*, Ins. no. 66 line 9 and foot-note.
98. *Ibid.*, Ins. no. 76 verse 16; 77 verse 12.
99. *Ibid.*, Ins. nos. 103-4 verse 2.
100. *Ibid.*, Ins. nos. 103-4 verse 3.
101. *Ibid.*, Ins. no. 51 verse 49.
102. *Ibid.*, Ins. nos. 63 line 29 and Appdx. 4 verse 27.
103. *Ibid.*
104. *CII*, IV. Ins. no. 74 line 34.
105. *Ibid.*, line 35.
106. *Ibid.*
107. *JBORS* vol. V, pt. II, pp. 583, 593.
108. *CII*, IV. Ins. no. 63 line 24 and Appdx. 4 verse 27.
109. *Ibid.*, Ins. no. 74 line 35.
110. *Ibid.*, Ins. no. 63 line 29.
111. *Ibid.*, Appdx. 4 verse 27.
112. *Ibid.*, Ins, nos. 12 verse 20; 13 line 9; 14 line 20; 74 line 38.
113. *CII*, III. p. 167
114. *Antiquities of Camba State* : pt. I, pp. 131-132.
115. *IA*, IX, p. 175, note 41.
116. *E.I.*, IX, p. 296.
117. *CII*, IV, pt. I, p. 43 fn. 9.
118. Altekar: *The Rashtrakutas and their Times* (1934), p. 233.
119. *Arthaśāstra*, B.K. I. 12.
120. *Śukra* I. 192.
121. *CII*, IV, Ins. no. 66 line 8.
122. *Ibid.*, Ins. no. 107 line 11.
123. *Ibid.*, Ins. nos. 116 line 9; 117 line 5.
124. *Ibid.*, Ins. no. 74 line 35.
125. A.K. Majumdar: *The Chalukyas of Gujarat*, p. 235.
126. Dasarath Sharma: *Early Chauhan Dynasties*, p. 205.
127. *CII*, IV, Ins. no. 74 line 35.
128. *Ibid.*, pt. IL, p. 396 fn. I.

129. *Ibid.*, Ins. no. 74 line 35.
130. U.N. Ghoshal: *Studies in Indian History and Culture.*
131. *Indian Culture,* vol. VII, p. 318.
132. *Journal Bihar Orissa Research Society*, vol. V, pp. 588 and 593.
133. *CII*, IV. Ins. no. 116 line 8.
134. *Ibid.*, Ins. no. 117 line 5.
135. *Ibid.*, Ins. no. 116 and 117.
136. *Ibid.*, Ins. no. 13 line 17 and 14 line 18. Also Mitra, S.K., *op.cit.*, p. 162.
137. *Ibid.*, Ins. no. 74 line 35.
138. *Ibid.*, Ins. no. 72 line 9.
139. *Ibid.*, Ins. no. 74 line 34.
140. *Ibid.*, Ins. no. 72 line 9.

## CHAPTER VII

# THE TREASURY *(KOŚA)*

The importance of the Treasury has constantly been emphasized upon in ancient Indian works on polity.[1] The same seems to have been kept in view in the Revenue Administration of the different dynasties ruling over Central India during the early medieval period. The principal means of fill in the treasury is taxation. The terms used for taxes are often found different from region to region and hence it is desirable to discuss them dynasty-wise.

Inscription of the Paramāras of Malwa supply us the following list of taxes levied:

**Bhāga**

*Bhāga* was the king's customary share of the produce, which was traditionally fixed at 1/6 of the produce, but the rate could be altered as stated in the legal texts.[2]

**Bhoga**

*Bhoga* denoted the periodic offerings of fruits, firewoods, flowers, milk and curd, which the subjects had to make to the king or to his local agents.[3]

**Uparikara**

*Uparikara* has been interpreted as additional fees or

tax which was to be given by the temporary tenants[4] or petty taxes payable in kind.[5] V.V. Mirashi's interpretation however seems to be better who thinks that *uparikara* meant 'an additional tax' which might have included the miscellaneous taxes in kind which the traders and the artisans had to pay.[6]

**Hiryaṇya**

*Hiraṇya* was perhaps a tax on some of the land produce which being perishable could not conveniently be put into share and had therefore to be paid in cash in contra-distinction to the rest which were paid in kind.[7]

**Śulka**

*Śulka* perhaps was next only to *bhoga* as a source of the royal revenue. Different authors have recommended different rates of *śulka*. Yājñavalkya states that the king is entitled to 1/20th part as *śulka* because he fixes the price of the articles.[8] The *Agni Purāṇa* goes a step further in prescribing a higher rate of *śulka* on foreign merchants. Its recommendation is that so much *śulka* should be levied on goods as would leave the merchant a profit of 5% only.[9] *Śulka* was of two types : (a) what was levied on goods carried by the land and collected at the *maṇḍapikā* and for this reason was known as *maṇḍapikādāya*[10] and (b) what was levied on the goods carried by water[11] and was called *ghaṭṭadāya.*[12]

That *maṇḍapikādāya* or octroi duty was prevalent in the Paramāra kingdom is proved by the Arthuna inscription of 1080 A.D. which refers to the following duties the income of which was granted to the deity:[13]

(i) one *varṇikā* on each *bharaka* of can died sugar and jaggery;

(ii) one *rūpaka* on each *bharaka* of Bengal madder, thread and cotton;

(iii) one coconut on every *bharaka* of cocoanuts;

(iv) one *mānaka* on every *mūṭaka* of salt;

(v) one nut from every 1000 areca-nuts;

(vi) one *palikā* for every *ghaṭaka* of butter and sesame oil;

(vii) 1 *rūpakas* on each *koṭikā* of clothing fabric;

(viii) two *pūlakas* on every *jāla* (*i.e.* bunch of buds);

(ix) two *santas* on each *lagaḍa* (a bar of gold, silver or other metal);

(x) a *pāṇaka* on each *karṣa* of oil;

(xi) a *vṛṣa-viṁśopaka* on each load of cattle-fodder;

(xii) one *dramma* on every pile of sugar;

(xiii) a *hāraka* of barley on a water-wheel;

(xiv) one *chaṅga* on every *bharaka* of loaded grain;

(xv) one citron on each *lagaḍā* and.

(xvi) a *vāpa* (a handful) on a *mūṭaka* or *āṭavika* of barley.[14]

The existence of *ghaṭṭadāya* or ferry. duties in the riverine areas can be inferred from the Bhopal inscription of Arjunavarman.[15] These duties may have been collected by an Officer known as the *Ghaṭṭapati.*[16]

That excise duty was levied in the Paramāra dominions is proved by the Arthuna inscription which refers to the levying of four *rūpakas* on each *vuṁvaka* of the distillers in the Paramāra kingdom.[17]

**Mārgādāya**

The road cess was known as *mārgādāya.*[18] The practice of collecting tolls land road cess for using highways was current among the Cāḷukya,[19] Gahaḍavāla[20] and Chāhamānas.[21] That it was imposed by the Paramāra kings is evidenced by the Panhera inscription, wherein we are told that king Jayasiṁha I assessed one *viṁśopaka* coin on every bull that passed through the road.[22] The Shergarh inscription informs us that Varaṅga, who was a *Mārgādāye-kauptika*[23], made a donation of five *vṛṣabhas* (a type of coin) out of the *mārgādāya* in 1018 A.D. in favour of God Somanātha for the purpose of providing incense and sandal in the temple.[24]

**Trade Tax**

The prevalence of trade tax is vouched for by the Arthuna inscription which refers to the levy of a *dramma* for the month on the shops of the braziers during the month of *Caitra* and one *dramma* each on the house of the traders in the local bazar the occasion of the *Caitra* festival and the festival of sacred thread.[25] Likewise, a *dramma* was levied on each traders' association.[26]

**Tax on Gambling**

The Paramāras seem to have levied a tax on gambling. The Arthuna inscription informs us that two *rūpakas* were levied on every gambling house in the Banswara state.[27]

**House Tax**

House tax was also known in the Paramāra dominions. The Arthuṇa inscription informs us that every house of the whole population was taxed at the rate of one *dramma* each in the state.[28] House tax is also referred to in the Bhopal inscription of king Arjunavarman.[29]

**Colapikā**

Another tax was *colapikā*.[30] It may have been an impost of fifty leaves or so on every *colapikā* brought from outside the town. In the Patanārāyaṇa inscription we are told that Rājaputra Gaṅgū and Karmasimha granted the revenue of *colapikā* in the village of Maḍaulī for twelve *ekādaśīs* for the maintenance of the temple of Paṭanārāyaṇa.[31]

**Śaṁhalātama(ka) – Samanvita**

*Śaṁhalātama(ka) – samanvita* is a new revenue term which occurs in the Mandhata inscription of king Devapāla[32], and is not met with anywhere else. We are unable to offer any explanation for it.

**Salt Tax**

Salt tax is referred to in the Bhopal inscription of Arjunavarman.[33]

**Other Taxes**

These levies plus the tributes from the feudatories and the war booty which were pouring in the Paramāra treasury must have enriched the Paramāra monarchs to a considerable extent. Besides, the king also received money by way of fines or *Daṇḍa* impose upon the wrong doer.[34] The ruler perhaps had the right to exact forced labour.[35] The property of the man who died without a male issue and without making adequate arrangements for succession to his property, escheated to the ruler. The king was at the same time the master of all marshy land, woodland and jungles, mines and salt-pits, mango and *madhuka* groves, treasure troves and the like.[36] The

Paramāra king may have also received *rājabhāvya* and different *bhāvyas* which the people had to pay for the services of the officers like the *Talāra* and the *Balādhipa.*[37]

As for the Candella kingdom of Jejākabhukti, it appears from the references supplied by their inscriptions that the sources of revenue exploited were identical with those known in many other parts of the contemperaray India. The terms found in their records comprise *Bhāga, Bhoga, Kara, Paśu, Hiraṇya, Daṇḍādaya, Cāṭa-dipraveśa* and *Śulka* and these were known to the territories of the Paramāras and Kalachuris and therefore need no detailed discussion

Many new terms of taxation occur in the inscriptions of the Kalachuris in addition to *Bhāgabhogakara* and *Hiraṇya* already diuscussed above. These are :

**Khala-bhikṣā and Marganaka**

This *Khala-bhikṣā* appearing in the Kairitala Stone Inscription of Lakṣamaṇarāja II[38] and Bargaon Stone Inscription of Śabara,[39] means, according to Dr. Ghosal "begging from the thrashing floor which stands for the demand for a portion of the crop, over and above the usual grain share that was collected from the grain heaped-upon the thrashing floor."[40] On the authority of Wilson, he compares the term with *Khaḷapuñji, i.e.* "the small heaps of grain taken from each larger pile at the time of measurement and under Maratha rule considered as a perquisite of the State."[41] This tax was levied probably to meet any special purpose or emergency. The second term *Mārgaṇaka* appearing in the Kumbhi Plates of Vijayasiṁha,[42] acccording to Ghoshal, "may be connected with the expression *mārganna* or a beggar and is apparently a benevolence of a more general character levied upon the villages."[43] It is interesting to note that Kauṭilya require a king to beg (*yāceta*) of the people to offer additional contribution.[44] The term also occurs in a land grant of Mathanadeva, a feudatory chief of the Pratihāras.[45]

**Pravaṇikara**

This tax is referred to in the Jabalpur Plates of Jayasiṁha[46], Rewa Stone Inscription of Vijayasiṁha[47] and the Kumbhi Plates of Vijayasiṁha.[48] The term is difficult to explain and, therefore, divergent opinions have been given. According to Dr. Tripathi, it was a tax on turnpikes intended to preserve the peace of the village by discouraging the "advent of a large number of visitors."[49] According to Dr. Mirashi, "*Pravaṇi* seem to meant *Śreṣṭhin*[50], a banker, for, as pointed out by Kielhorn, he appears with *Vaṇika* in the Rajor Inscription of Mathanadeva".[51] The tax, thus, appears to be imposed on dealers or bankers. The term also appears in most of the inscriptions of the Gāhaḍavālas and the Somavaṁśī kings of Trikaliṅga.[52]

**Trade Taxes**

*Śulka* is a term generally used in ancient Indian literature to indicate all kinds of tolls and duties imposed for carrying out trade. Kauṭilya whose definition of the term is most extensive, means by it "duties levied upon articles imported into the city, port dues, customs collected by the ferrymen and boundary – officers, duty upon mining products, duty upon imported salt, duty upon animals intended for slaughter etc."[53] The term See

Ms. (customs officer) apperas in the Kahla Plates of Sodhadeva of (V) E 1135.[54]

A fair idea of the different types of duties imposed for carrying on trade can be obtained from the Bilahari Stone Inscription of Yajvarājadeva II as follows :

"In the *Maṇḍapikā* (*i.e.* custom house) of the town there shall be paid a *Ṣoḍaśikā* (coin) on (every) *Khaṇḍikā* of salt and (also) one *Ṣoḍaśikā* for every oil-mill per month and a *paura* for a couple of *yugās* per day.

In case of betel nuts, black-pepper, dried-ginger and other merchandise a *paura* (shall be paid) by every measurer (*bharaka*); a *kapardi* shall be paid for every *vīthī* (*i.e.* shop) and *dyūtakapardas* for vegetables and egg-plants.

In case of dealers in liquids the tax should be (in the form of) bundles of grass, *dhīmara* and whatever (else may be possible). An elephant (offered for sale) should be taxed four *pauras*, and a horse two *pauras.*"[55]

The Karitalai Stone Inscription of Lakṣmaṇarāja II gives further details by supplying the following information.

"He always gave a jar *(ghaṭī)* (of corn) for every *goṇī*, and also a couple of *ṣoḍaśīs* (i.e. *karṣa*).

The *Deśai* offered one and a half times the one-twenty second portion of the five spirituous liquors and a quarter of the goods carried (into the town) among (these) donations.

And the chief of the *Vāgūlikas* gave (a bundle of) fifty leaves. The *Pāyaṭis* gave another (bundle of) fifty leaves. And the whole *Maṇḍala* gave the alms at four thrashing floors."[56]

**Viṣayadāna**

This tax which is referred to in the Jabalpur Plates of Jayasiṁha of (K) E. 918,[57] according to Dr. Tripathi[58] and Dr. Mirashi,[59] must have been some kind of district tax. It is noteworthy that *Viṣayadānika,* as an officer, has been referred to in the Kahla Plates of Sodhadeva of (V) E. 1135.[60]

**Paṭṭakiladāya**

This was probably the village headman's dues. It has been referred to in the Jabalpur Plates of Jayasiṁha of (K) E. 918, and the Kumbhi Plates of Vijayasiṁha of KE 932.[61]

**Dussādhyadāya**

This tax, according to Hiralal was imposed "for mending the incorrigibles". The salary of *Duṣṭasādhaka*[62] (mentor of criminals) was probably paid out of this. It has been referred to in the Jabalpur Plates of Jayasiṁha and the Kumbhi Plates of Vijayasiṁha.[63]

**Vāḍa**

This fiscal term appearing in the Jabalpur Plates of Jayasiṁha of (K)E. 918 and the Kumbhi Plates of Vijayasiṁha[64], has been interpreted by Hiralal (who reads *Pravanivāda* together) as – "dues for occupying camping grounds."[65] The term, however, appears alone in the Kumbhi Plates and as such is inexplicable in the present state of knowledge.

**Carī**

This was the grazing tax which has been referred to in the Jabalpur Plates of Jayasiṁha.[66]

**Rasavatī**

This was the excise duty, the tax imposed on liquor, which has been referred to in the Jabalpur Plates of Jayasiṁha and the Kumbhi Plates of Vijayasiṁha.[67]

**Kāmata**

This fiscal term appears again in the two above mentioned inscriptions.[68] *Kāmata*, according to Hiralal "was a rigid form of home-farm which is still referred to in law-books but has become practically obsolete."[69]

**Viṣenimādāya**

This term referred to again in the above mentioned two inscriptions[70] appears as *viseṇā* in the Rewa Stone Inscription of Vijayasiṁha.[71] According to Hiralal, it was the fore-runner of the modern dues for crossing river.[72]

**Mavāḍa and Ardha-puruṣārikadāya**

These two fiscal terms, appearing respectively in the Rewa Stone Inscription and the Kumbhi Plates of Vijayasiṁha are inexplicable in the present state of knowledge.

**Revenue from mines and treasure trove**

The State derived income from the working of the mines and the treasure troves. The inscriptions of the Kalachuris frequently refer to the mines of iron and salt (*lohalavaṇākara*)[73] and treasures and deposits (*nidhinikṣepa*)[74] incomes from which is said to have been transferred to the donees.

**Revenue from fines**

Fines paid by the convicted persons were an additional source of income of the State. The Amoda Plates of Pṛthvīdeva I of (K)E. 831, refers to the fine imposed on illegal distillation (*rasavatidaṇḍa*).[75] Receipts from fines (*daṇḍādāya*) has been referred to in the Banaras Plates of (K)E. 723.[76] The Kumbhi Plates of Vijayasiṁha also refer to the fines (*daṇḍa*) in general.[77]

**Tributes from Feudatories**

Annual tributes paid by the feudatories to their respective overlord was also a source of income to the State. Payment of tributes by the feudatories of the Kalachuri kings has been referred to in a number of their inscriptions.[78]

No reference is available in the inscriptions of Kalachuris to indicate the principles of taxation.

We do not possess any specific account about the way the king spent his money. A good deal must have gone to the Brāhmaṇa donees, temples, monasteries, scholars and poets, and a considerable amount would have been spent on the warlike activities of the rulers. The *Mānasollāsa* suggests that the king should spend ordinarily 3/4 of the yearly revenue and save 1/4.

REFERENCES

1. *Arthaśāstra* II, 1.8; *Kāmandaka* XIII. 33; *Viṣṇudharmottara* II. 61.17; *Manu* VII.65 etc.
2. We do not have any information from the Paramāra sources regarding the rate of *bhāga*. Neither Lakṣmīdhara nor Someśvara lay down any specific rate

at which the land revenue was to be collected. The latter simply says that 1/6, 1/8 or 1/12 of the share of the produce should be collected *as bhāga (Mānaso,* I, *Vim,* II, vv. 113-47).

3. *AR,* pp. 212-16, Ghoshal, U.N.; *op. cit.,* p. 290.
4. *Ibid.,* p. 299.
5. *AR,* pp. 214-15.
6. *CII,* IV, Intro., p. cxli ; V.V. Mirashi along with A.S. Altekar thinks that *uparikara* and *bhoga* were one and the same tax. But as both these terms are used together in the Paramāra records, it proves that they were separate taxes.
7. That *hiraṇya* was paid in cash is suggested by *Prabandhacintāmaṇi* (p. 53) and the Baroda grant of Dhruva II.
8. *Yājña, Vyāvahtiriadhyāya,* v. 261.
9. *Agni Purāṇa, Adh,* XXIII, vv. 23-24.
10. In the Shergarh inscription of 1017 A.D. (*EI,* XXIII, p. 140) we are informed that the merchants Narasiṁha, Govṛṣa and Thirāditya made a daily gift of a *karṣa* of ghee to Bhaṭṭāraka Nagnaka out of the *maṇḍapikādāya.*
11. *Mitākṣarā on Yājña, Vyavahārādhyāya,* v. 263.
12. *JAOS,* VII, p. 27.
13. *EI,* XIV, pp. 295-310.
14. *Ibid.,* pp. 302-03, vv. 69-81.
15. *JAOS,* VII, p. 27.
16. *CII,* Intro., p. cxlii; *ibid.,* Ins. no. 74, v. 34.
17. *EI,* XIV, p. 302, v. 74.
18. *EI,* XXIII, p. 140.
19. *Rās Mālā,* p. 235: IA, VI, p. 204.
20. *EI,* XIV, pp. 194-95.
21. *EI,* XI, pp. 59-60.
22. *EI,* XXI, p. 48, vv. 44-45.

23. He was officer in charge for collecting tolls and road cess.
24. *EI*, XXI. p. 140.
25. *EI*, XIV, p. 302, vv.73-74.
26. *Ibid.*, v. 77.
27. *Ibid.*, v. 75.
28. *EI*, XIV, p. 302, v. 75.
29. *JAOS*, VII, p. 27.
30. Referred to in the Paṭanārāyaṇa inscription of the Paramāra ruler Pratāpasiṁha. *IA*, XLV, p. 79.
31. *Ibid.*
32. *EI*, IX, p. 112, ll. 72-73.
33. *JAOS*, VII, p. 27.
34. Altekar, A.S., *op. cit.*, p. 281.
35. *Ibid.*, p. 280.
36. *Ibid.*, p. 282.
37. *Ibid.*
38. *CII*, IV, Ins. no. 42 verse 42. It refers to alms at four thrashing floors.
39. *Ibid.*, Ins. no. 43 line 3 and fn. 1.
40. *Hindu Revenue System*, p. 327.
41. *Ibid.*, fn. 2.
42. *CII*. IV. Appdx. 4 verse 27.
43. *Hindu Revenue System*, p. 231.
44. *Arthaśāstra* V. p. 271.
45. *EI*, III, pp. 263 ff.
46. *CII*, IV. Ins. no. 63 line 29.
47. *Ibid.*, Ins. no.7 line 16.
48. *Ibid.*, Appdx. 4 verse 21.
49. *History of Kanauj*, p. 349.
50. *CII*, IV, p. 331 fn.2.
51. *EI*, III, p.263 fn
52. *Ibid.*, XI, pp. 47.
53. *Arthaśāstra*, II. 22
54. *CII*, IV, Ins. no. 34.

55. *CII,* IV, Ins. no. 45 verse 79-81.
56. *CII,* IV, Ins. no. 42 verses 39-42.
57. *Ibid.*, Ins. no. 63. line 30.
58. *History of Kanauj,* p. 349.
59. *CII,* IV, p. 334.
60. *Ibid.*, Ins. no. 74 line 35.
61. *Ibid.*, Ins. no. 63 line 29 and Appdx. 4 verse 27.
62. *Ibid.*, Appdx. 4 verse 27.
63. *Ibid.*, Ins. no. 63 line 29 and Appdx. 4 verse 27.
64. *Ibid.*
65. *EI,* XXI, p. 93.
66. *CII,* IV, Ins. no. 63 line 29.
67. *Ibid.*, Ins. nos. 63 line 29 and Appdx. 4 verse 27.
68. *Ibid.*
69. *EI,* XXI, p. 93.
70. *Ibid.*
71. *CII,* IV, Ins. no. 70. line 14.
72. *EI,* XXI, p. 93.
73. *CII,* IV, Ins. nos. 56 line 22, 23; 63 line 28; 65 line 2, Appdx. 4 V.I.; Appdx. 2, V. 27 etc.
74. *Ibid.*, Ins. nos. 65 line 13; 69 line 9.
75. *Ibid.*, Ins. no. 76 line 32.
76. *Ibid.*, Ins. no. 48 line 43.
77. *Ibid.*, Appdx. 4 verse 27.
78. *Ibid.*, Ins. nos. 48 verse 10; 77 Verse 23; Appdx. 5 V. 4 etc.

## CHAPTER VIII

# ARMY *(BALA)* AND FORT *(DURGA)*

### A. ARMY *(BALA)*

That strong armies were kept ready by the ruling dynasties of Central India during the early medieval period can not be denied. The wars and couquests often conducted by them, as shown in their respective histories, are unmistakable proof of the strength of their armies and superiority of their organisations. The supreme leadership lay in the hands of the kings themselves. They often led the army personally in military campaigns. The ministers in charge of war and peace *(sāndhivigrahika*) or *Sāndhivigraha – mahāsaciva*) was evidently the political adviser to the king in military matters relating to the declaration of war and settlement of terms of peace.

Inscription of the Candellas provide us the information that the Army had its Commander-in-chief designated as *Senāpati*[1], who must have led the forces in the battle-field. Besides, there were special officers in charge of elephants and cavalry, *hastyaśvanetā.*[2] The defensive organisation was also looked after by specially appointed officers. The *Purabalādhyakṣa* was the Superintendent of the forces defending the capital city.

*Koṭṭapāla* referred to in the Dhureti Copper Plate, may be regarded as the Officer in charge of defence of small towns. The office of the *Ekaśvagoptā* also appears to have been a military one. His duty was to protect properties, *i.e.* buildings etc., under the control of the army. It may be noted that the functions of the *Purabalādhyakṣa* and the *Ekaśvagoptā* are found to have been combined and entrusted to the same officer. The forts must have had a governor (*durgādhipa*). Paṁsuha, son of Śrī Ayo, is mentioned to have been appointed as a governor of Jayadurga along with its approach roads (*pratolikānvita Jayapura-durgādhipa*).[3] The office of the governor of the fort was called *durgādhikāra*. Ānanda, the younger brother of Vāseka, the *Viśiṣa* of Jayapura, is stated to have been made the governor of the fort by the king.[4] The *Aśvavaidya* or the Veterinary Surgeon, mentioned in the Candella record[5], must have been attached to the army.

Even Kāyasthas and Brāhmaṇas were entrusted with responsible military functions. Jaunādhara and Mālādhara, younger brothers of Gaṅgādhara belonged to the Vāstavya Kāyastha family, which, as already mentioned, produced illustrious administrators. Both the brothers have been described as distinguished warriors (*vīramukhya*). The Pachār Plate refers to Senāpati Madanapālaśarman, evidently a Brāhmaṇa. In recognition of meritorious military services grants of land were used to be made in their favour. Madanapālaśarman received the grant of a village, as recorded in the Pachār Plate of the time of Paramārdi. The Dahi Grant refers to one Mallaya as a distinguished soldier being similarly rewarded.[6] The Charkhari Plate of Vīravarman records the grant of a village to one Rāuta Abhi for a deed of valour in the battle of Sondhi (*Sondhisaṁgrāma...kṛta-viryātiśayo prasāde*).[7] There was also the system of granting pension, '*Mṛtyukavṛtti*', to heirs of persons killed in battle. The Garra Plates of V.S. 1261 (1205-1206 A.D.) record grants of lands to Rāuta Sāmanta, son of Rāuta Pāpe, who was killed at Kakaḍaḍaha in a battle with the Turuskas.[8]

As far as the military system of the Paramāras of Malwa is concerned, we come to know from their inscriptions and contemporary literary evidences that their army consisted of two types of soldiers *viz.*, *Maulas* and *Bhṛtas*. The *Mūlas* were hereditary and depended for their livehood on land grants made by the king. The *Bhṛtas* were paid wages. Of these two, the Maulas were more reliable and were preferred to the *Bhṛtas*, who changed sides where they received higher wages form the other party.

The army at this time was divided into three main branches, namely infantry, cavalry, and elephants. Bhoja, in his *Yuktikalpataru*, mentions the importance of these different branches of the army. According to him, foot soldiers are the main source of strength on all occasions.[9] He was not ignorant of the importance of cavalry, as he refers to the horses from Tajikistan and Tushāra Countries as the best.[10] Elephants formed an important source of military strength, and they accompanied the army on almost all important occasions. Chariots, though not important, were still in use as they are referred to in the *Yuktikalpataru*.[11] When the Paramāras conquered Lāṭa, the importance of maintaining a navy was felt. It is for this reason that Bhoja, in his *Yuktikalpataru*[12], gives elaborate directions for constructing different types of ships. He further says that the king, who has boats, wins the war.

The army was under the charge of military officers. *Mahādaṇḍanāyaka* or *Daṇḍanāyaka* was probably the highest military officer, identified with a commander-in-chief. Srī Chandra, who was *Daṇḍanāyaka*, was probably in charge of the region round Bhilsa.[13] *Balādhikṛta*[14] was put in charge of the military town. *Sādhanika*[15] appears to have been in charge of cavalry and, was perhaps stationed at important forts. *Mahāmātra*[16] was the commander of the elephant forces.

For the protection of the civic population, proper attention was given to the construction of forts and walled cities. The famous forts of this time were Dhārā, Maṇḍapadurga and Kośavardhana. Bhoja, in his *Samarāṅgaṇasūtradhāra*,[17] suggests methods of constructing various types of forts.

The soldiers had peculiar dresses and weapons. They were heavily clad, with helmet and iron nets protecting separately, the belly, thighs, arms, and other parts of the body. They also wore pugrees, made up with multi-coloured scarves arranged in layers. They used swords, discs, daggers, spears, bows, *śūla* and *parigha* as their weapons.

The *yātrā* or march of the army, was an occasion of great significance.People celebrated this event with great rejoicings as is clear from the Banswara Copper Plate of Bhoja.[18] Dasharatha Sharma[19] thinks that '*Koṅkaṇa-vijaya-parva*' may mean the *Koṅkaṇa–vijaya-yātrā-parva, i.e.* the day on which the Paramāra forces started on their expedition for the conquest of Koṅkaṇa. Dhanapāla[20] gives a vivid description of the army on march.

About the Kalachuris a better picture about the organisation of army is obtained from their inscriptions.

**The four-fold division of Army**

The army of the Kalachuris consisted of the traditional four-fold forces *(caturaṅgabalam)* often met with in the Sanskrit texts. These were chariots, elephants, horses and foot-soldiers. The inscriptions of the Kalachuris which refer to the four-membered army are: The Khairha Plates of Yaśaḥkarṇa of (K)E. 823[21], the Karanbel Stone Inscription of Jayasiṁha[22] and the Akaltara Stone Inscription of Ratnadeva II.[23]

**Chariots**

It has often been suggested[24] that chariots ceased to be used in ancient Indian warfare from 8th century onwards, for, neither there is indication of it in the contemporary literature nor in the writings of the Muslim historians. The army of the Kalachuris seems to be no exception to this. Though chariot seems to have been continued for other purposes, no reference to its use in the battlefield appears in the inscriptions of the Kalachuris. The ideal of *caturaṅgabala* probably continued only in theory, for, wherever we come across reference to the different units of the army, we find conspicuous absence of reference to the chariots. This may be noticed in a number of Kalachuri inscriptions which refer to elephants, horses and foot-soldiers as constituents of the army.[25]

**Elephants**

Elephants played a prominent role in all ancient Indian warfare.[26] Ancient Indian thinkers like Kauṭilya[27] and Kāmandaka[28] and works like Nītivākyāmṛta[29] and *Agnipurāṇa*[30] constantly emphasize upon the importance of elephants in army. That this was put into practice by the Kalachuri rulers also is amply evidenced by a number of references in their inscriptions.[31] Most important among these are references to "battles which were dreadful with clashes of marching arrays of elephants"[32], "huge scent elephants in army"[33], "arrays of elephants of kings killed by their host soldiers",[34] "mountains which were his elephants"[35] etc. The Ratanpur Stone Inscriptions of Vāhara of (K) E. 1552 records that at the time of the issue of the record, "a thousand horses together with sixty elephants, more lustrous than fire and destructive of foes in battle"[36], were stationed at Ratanpur. Prof. Hodivala would have us believe that Gāṅgeyadeva, who was contemporary of Sultan Mahmud of Ghazni, possessed one thousand elephants.[37] The importance of the elephant force is reflected in the Kharod Stone inscription of Ratnadeva III of Cedi in year 933 which states that among various factors responsible for weakening the Kalachuri empire, the weak elephant force of the country was one.[38]

For the Kalachuris, the main source of procuring elephants for their army seems to be forest of the Vindhyas. This is indicated in the Akaltara Stone Inscription of Ratnadeva II, which points out that "being vehemently fond of the sport of capturing elephants on the earth, he (*i.e.* Vallabharāja) has made the whole Vindhya forest devoid of elephants.[39] After their capture, these elephants were brought to the capital through their drivers. The Kosgain Stone Inscription (no. 1) of Vāhara states that "having captured at will wild elephants which had been sporting freely, he got them brought by their drivers to his capital from Ratnapura."[40] Training and care of such captured elephants was an important aspect which made the elephants fit for being sent to the battle-fields. That perfect science for the same existed is indicated in the Karitalai Stone Inscription of Lakṣmaṇarāja II and the Koni Stone Inscription which refer respectively to Prime Minister Someśvara being matchless in the "science of care and examination of elephants and horses" (*hastyaśvapālanaparīkaṣaṇa karmaśāstra*)[41] and Kāsala being conversant in the "science of elephants" (*hastyāyurveda*).[42] Rājaśekhara also refers to the "training of elephants" (*hastiśikṣā*).[43] These well-trained elephants, driven by drivers with the help of *aṅkuśa* were well-decorated before being sent to battle-fields. With their regulated movements, the arrays of decorated elephants presented a picturesque view, a graphic description of which appears in the *Bālarāmāyaṇa* of Rājaśekhara as follows:

> "Arrays of elephants with waving ensigns are advancing to attack, their throats uttering the sounds of pride and defiance that boy them up with drums beating loud-the regulated movements with which they rapidly fall into the lines of battle are beautiful to behold, the riders sit conspicuous upon them, their heads are straight and set in a line by the waving of the sharp goads while all points of space are covered with the rutting juice drizzling unceasingly from them."[44]

Apart from the driver, mounted on these elephants used to be the kings, generals and warriors who used to fight with bows and arrows. Mounted archery from the back of elephants was an ancient Indian practice[45] which seems to have been continued by the Kalachuris in their warfare. The Sheorinarayan Stone Inscription of Jājalladeva II of Cedi year 919 states that "mounted on the elephant Mānasiddhi, he (*i.e.* Ulhaṇadeva) who wielded in his hand, a dreadful bow, routed the army of the king of Cedi with (his) arrows".[46] The Khajuraho inscription, recording the victory of Candella. Yaśovarman over the Cedi ruler (Yuvarāja I ? ) states that "he was protected by multitudes of angry and invincible bowmen riding elephants in rut."[47] All these indicate the important role that elephants played in the army of the Kalachuris.

**Cavalry**

Cavalry formed an important division of ancient Indian army. Importance of cavalry was strongly emphasized upon by Somadeva[48] (10th cent. A.D.) and Someśvara[49] (12th century A.D). That Kalachuris followed the foot-steps of their ancestors is evidenced by a number of references like "ocean of horses"[50], "hundreds of hoofs of numerous galloping horses"[51], "wave-like rows of horses",[52] "dust raised by the pairs of hard hooves of the crores of horses in his army"[53] etc., available in their inscriptions. As noted above, the Ratanpur Stone Inscription of Vāhara records the stationing of one thousand horses at Ratanpur, the capital. The Rewa Stone Inscription of Karṇa of (K) E. 812 states that his general Vappulla fought a battle of horses (*ghoṭakavigraha*) at the foot of Yellow Mountain (*pītaparavata*) and defeated the army of Trilochana.[54] Liking that military generals and kings had for this animal is indicated in the Pujaripali Stone Inscription of Gopāladeva which states that Gopāla "appears in every place mounted on a horse like

Revanta."[55] No reference is available in the inscriptions to indicate the source of the acquisition of horses. That horses were well-looked-after according to the science of care and examination of horses has already been noted above.

**Infantry**

The infantry, *i.e.* foot-soldiers formed the largest in the army. The inscriptions refer to "thousands of stream-like battalions"[56], "ocean of forces"[57] "mass of dust raised by his forces"[58] etc. It seems that the Kalachuris had two main kinds of armies *viz.*, the standing army maintained by the Central government with regular pay, food, clothing etc., and the feudal levies, an irregular force maintained by the feudatories which came to the help of the Central government at short notice. The Bilhari Stone Inscription of Yuvarājdeva II refers to the "elephants and horses, powerful feudatories and foot-soldiers" of the powerful lord of the Cedi.[59] In addition to these two sources of procuring foot-soldiers, a third source is indicated in Rājaśekhara's reference to *'śastrajīvīs'* (people living on the profession of arms) in his *Kāvyamīmāṁsā.*[60] It seems that such people having profession of arms formed themselves into a guild or corporation. The fact that contemporary inscriptions like the Nāgardhan Plates of Svāmirāja[61] mentions a corporation of elephant drivers, testifies to the fact of the prevalence of such a system at that time. It may thus, be inferred that such guilds were the third source of supply of military to the Central government.

Regarding the problem of recruitment of different classes in the army, the orthodox theory of the four *varṇas* was, that military profession was the exclusive monopoly of a single caste *viz.* the Kṣatriya. That this was not put into actual practice is evident from the writings of authorities like Kauṭilya, Śukra etc., who enjoin the recruitment of all the four classes in army. According to Śukra[62], caste does not determine the quality of soldiers. They may be Śūdra, Kṣatriya, Vaiśya and Mlecchas or of mixed caste; but they must be brave and well disciplined. That this practice was also followed by the Kalachuris, is evidenced by several instances of military officers and generals who belonged to different castes. Glaring examples of Brāhmaṇa warriors in the army of the Kalachuris are those of Someśvara[63], (the Prime Minister of Lakṣamaṇarāja II), Ṭhakkura Sāhilla and his descendants[64], Puruṣottama, his ancestors and successors[65], *Daṇḍanāyaka* Jāgu etc.[66] Similarly, Jāṭa and his descendants *viz.* Yaśaḥpāla, Padmasiṁha, Chandrasiṁha, Kīrtisiṁha and Malayasiṁha who helped the Kalachuri kings by their military conquests were all Kṣatriyas.[67] Devarāja and his descendants[68] *viz.* Rāghava, Harigaṇa and Vallabharāja who were all military generals belonged to Vaiśya lineage. Similarly Someśvara of the Rewa Stone Inscription of Karṇa and his ancestors who were all ministers and warriors were Kāyasthas.[69] Śūdras, of whom we find no reference in the inscriptions must have formed the major part of the rank and file in the army. Thus, recruitment to the army of the Kalachuris was broad-based and service in it was thrown open to all classes of people. Regarding the different units in which the foot-soldiers must have been divided and put in charge of the officers, we do not have any reference in the inscriptions of the Kalachuris and other contemporary dunasties of Central India.

## B. FORT *(DURGA)*

The value of Fort as an important limb of military system was well recognised by ancient Indian political thinkers like Yājñavalkya, Bṛhaspati, and Kauṭilya etc. In the early medieval state also fort constituted an important element.

In the Bundelkhand region of Central India where the Candellas ruled, the importance of the Fort of Kālañjara, Ajaygarh, Mahoba etc. was never underestimated. The whole history of the dynasty has centred round the historic fort of Kālañjara and to a lesser degree, the fort of Ajaygarh. Time and again the fortune of the dynasty depended on the possession of Kālañjara. The extraordinary importance of forts in the Candella state was due to the geographical situation of the country and the method of warfare followed in that period. Dr. Kane rightly observes that "the capital mirrored the prosperity of the country and if properly walled also provided security".[70] Central India is mountainous, crossed by the ranges of the Vindhyas, Bhanrer and Kaimur, and the whole region is interlaced with innumerable rivers. The mountain fortresses of Ajaygarh, Mahoba and other places provided security for the state and its people and made access to the heart of the country very difficult. So, the physical features of the country gave unusual importance to the construction and maintenance of forts in the Candella kingdom and hence the kings paid much attention to this aspect of administration and national security. The Ajaygarh Stone inscription of Vīravarman praises Trailokyavarman as "a very creator in providing strong places (*durga pravidhānavedaḥ*)".[71] A minister of Kīrtivarman is recorded to have built the fort of Kīrtigiri.[72]

The forts were governed by an officer appointed by the king. The Ajaygarh Rock inscription of the time of Bhojavarman states that one Ānanda, born in the Vāstavya Kāyastha family of Jājuka, was appointed by Trailokya-varman as the governor of the fort of Jayapura (*Durgadhi-kāri*). Ānanda is credited for reducing to submission the wild tribes of Bhillas, Śabaras and Pulindas.[73]

Maheśvara, an ancestor of the same family, was thoroughly familiar with every branch of letters and possessed many other good qualities. After serving Kīrtivarman, he received the title of *Visisa* of Kālañjara along with the grant of a village from the king.[74] Ānanda's elder brother was called *Vase* for his excellent qualities and "the minds of the people as well as that of king Trailokyavarman were about to prove submissive to him". Considering him competent for the work, Trailokyavarman appointed him in the office of *Visisa* over the fort named Jaya, and gave him a village for ever. Vase built a beautiful temple and a tank. He is also praised for defeating and killing Bhojuka, an enemy of Trailokyavarman.[75]

The office of *Visisa* is not known to have been found in the inscriptions of any other dynasty. Dr. Ray believes it to be an administrative post, but he does not offer any suggestion as to the exact nature and duties of this officer.[76] The *Visisa* does not seem to have been a civil officer, for, both Maheśvara and Vase were appointed *Visisas* of the forts of Kālañjara and Ajaygarh and not of any administrative division. The *Visisa* cannot have been the governor of the fort, because the inscription specifically mentions Ānanda (Vase's brother) as the

*Durgadhikāri* of Ajaygarh fort. Dr. Altekar believes that in ancient Indian state there was probably an inspector-general of forts at the capital.[77] The *Visisas* of the Ajaygarh inscription may have had some such office, but on the other hand Vase appears to have been appointed over one fort only. It may well be that the rank of *Visisa* was rather a title of honour or a sinecure than governmental post.

In the territories of the Paramāras of Malwa the famous forts were Maṇḍapadurga, Kosavardhana and Dhārā. The fort of Dhārā was so impregnable that Jayasiṁha Siddharāja of Gujarat had taken 12 years to break it open and that too due to the treachery of a Malwa soldier. Lakṣmīdhara suggests that the forts should not be overcrowded by having therein unnecessary people.[78] Among the means of defence, it is interesting to note his advice that deadly cobras be thrown on the attacking enemy to check their advance.

As for the Kalachuris, their inscriptions refers to the forts of Piplām, Saraharāgadha, Machakā-Sihava, Kosaṅga and Kālañjara. The Alhaghat Stone Inscription of Narasiṁha of (V)E. 1216, refers to Chīhula the son of *Mahārāṇaka* of Piplām fort who caused the Ṣaṭaṣaḍikāghāṭa to be constructed and (a temple of) the goddess Ambika to be built near the road leading to it.[79] The location of the fort has not yet been identified. The Rajim Stone Inscription of Pṛthvīdeva II of (K)E. 896, records that Jagapāla, the military general of Ratnadeva II and Pṛthvīdeva II conquered the forts of Sarahāragaḍha (modern Sarangarh in Durg Dist. of Chhattisgarh) and Machaka-Sihavā (modern Mechka Sihava, south of Dhamtari in Raipur district of Chhattisgarh).[80] No details of either of these forts are available. The Kosgain Stone Inscriptions (no. I and II) of Vāhara, refer to the fort of Kosaṅga (same as modern Kosgain in Bilaspur district of Chhattisgarh) which was in possession of king Vāhara. The first Kosgain Inscription of Vāhara referring to the fort of Kosaṅga states it to be "high and invulnerable fort like another heaven on earth, which, like the ocean, receives clouds hospitably... (and) has (large) stores of various kinds of corn, wealth, fuel and grass accumulated in it..."[81] It states, further, that "having placed all wealth.... in this fort of many peaks (called) Kosaṅga, (and) having destroyed completely all hosts of enemies, this (Vāharendra) also roams about, marching here and there".[82] The first and the second Kosgain Inscription refer respectively to the construction of the main gate (*simhadvāra*) of the fort by Mādhava, a minister, and by Ghāṭamma, a feudatory of king Vāhara.[83] The remains of the fort as it exist to-day has been described in detail by Mr. Beglar in his Archaeological Survey Reports.[84] The fort of Kālañjara has been referred to in the Kahla Plates of Soḍhadeva which indicates its possession by the Kalachuris of Sarayūpāra.[85] That it was also conquered by Karṇa of Tripuri branch of the Kalachuris is hinted by Bilhaṇa who describes Karṇa as "death to the lord of Kālañjara".[86] The Khalari Stone Inscription of Haribrahmadeva of (V)E. 1470, refers to the conquest of eighteen fortresses by Simhaṇa.[87]

In addition to these epigraphic references of the forts, we know that the Ratanpur Stone Inscription of Pṛthvīdeva II of (V)E. 1207 and Raipur Stone Inscription of Brahmadeva of (V) E. 1458 were discovered from the forts of Ratanpur and Raipur respectively. Very little remains of these forts are existing today.

The Tahankāpār Plates of Pamparājadeva refer to a *Vaṇikoṭṭa*, a traders' fortress, which, according to Hiralal, was a fortified place probably made by the *banjārās* for storing grain purchased for transport.[88]

Forts, in ancient Indian literature, were mainly classified under four main heads *viz. sthaladurga* (fort built on land), *jaladurga* (fort surrounded water), *giridurga* (hill-fortress) and *vanadurga* (fort built in the midst of forests).[89] That this classification was known to the Kalachuris also, is hinted in the Gurgi Stone Inscription of Kokalladeva I, which refers to '*jaladurga*'.[90]

Regarding the siegecraft, the inscriptions of the Kalachuris do not supply us with any details. The fact that an impregnable fort like Kālañjara was in the possession of the Kalachuris, itself speaks of the strategy of siegecraft in which the Kalachuri army must bave been well-trained.

## REFERENCES

1. Senāpati Madanapālaśarman -Icchawar Plate., I.A., XXV, p. 205.
2. *E.I.*, I, p. 20, v. 30.
3. *Ibid.*, XXVIII, p. 104, l. 20. Ajaygarh R. I. of Kīrtivarman records the conferment of the authority over the gates of the Kālañjara fort (*Kālañjaradvāravarādhikāram*) upon Maheśvara, *Ibid.*, XXX, p. 88.
4. *EI*, I, p. 335., v. 22.
5. *A.S.R.*, XXI., p. 51.
6. *Ibid.*, pp. 74-76.
7. *E.I.*, XX., p. 133.
8. *Ibid.*, pp. XVI, pp. [illegible] ff.
9. *Yuktikalpataru*, p. 7.

10. *Ibid.*, p. 182.
11. *Ibid.*, p. 7.
12. *Ibid.*, pp. 224-29.
13. *CII.* VII, pp. 122-25.
14. *Tilakamañajarī*, p. 97.
15. *Ibid.*, p. 150.
16. *Ibid.*, p. 149.
17. *Samarāṅgaṇasūtradhāra*, p. 36.
18. *EI.*, I, p. 182.
19. *Jour. Ganaganath Jha Institute*, V, pp. 61ff.
20. *Tilakamañjarī*, p. 96.
21. *CII*, IV, Ins. No. 56 verse 8.
22. *Ibid.*, Appdx. 3, verse 53.
23. *Ibid.*, Ins. no. 84, verse 19.
24. Dikshitar; *War in Ancient India*, p. 166; Chakaravarti, P.C., *The Art of War in Ancient India* (1934), p. 248.
25. *CII*, IV, Ins. nos. 45 verse 59; 51 verse 28; 88 verse 19 and 25 etc.
26. B.P. Sinha, *PIHC*, 1955, pp., 51-57 (*Elephants in Ancient Indian Army*).
27. *Arthaśāstra*, BK. 2, ch. 2.
28. *Kām.*, XVI, 10-12.
29. *Nītivākyāmṛta*, pp. 82-83.
30. *Agnipurāṇa*, 287, 5-6.
31. *CII*, IV, Ins. nos. 45 verse 47,62, 69; 50 verse 24, 25; 51 verse 19, 23 etc.
32. *Ibid.*, Ins. no.74, v. 13.
33. *Ibid.*, Ins. no.50.v.9.
34. *Ibid.*, Ins. no. 51 verse 19.
35. *Ibid.*, verse 23.
36. *Ibid.*, Ins. nos. 103-4 verse 1.
37. Hodivala, *Studies in Indo-Muslim History*, pp. 73 ff.
38. *CII*, IV, Ins. no. 100, verse 25.
39. *Ibid.*, Ins. no. 84 verse 17.

40. *Ibid.*, Ins. no. 105 verse.10.
41. *Ibid.*, Ins. no. 42 verse 8.
42. *Ibid.*, Ins. no. 90 verse 37,
43. *Kāvyamīmāṁsā* of Rājaśekhara. Ed. by C. D. Dalal and B.A. Sastri (G.O.S) 1934, p. 40, line 9.
44. *Bālarāmāyaṇa*, Act. II, *śloka* 58.
45. Vide, P.K. Gode, *Collected Works*, vol. V.
46. *CII*, IV, Ins. no. 98, verse 28.
47. *EI*, I, p. 127.
48. *Nītivākyāmṛta*, pp. 83-4.
49. *Mānas*. I. 81 verse 574.
50. *CII*, IV, Ins. no. 67. verse 19.
51. *Ibid.*, Ins. no. 73 verse 30.
52. *Ibid.*, Ins. no. 98 verse 25.
53. *Ibid.*, Ins. no. 105 verse 12.
54. *Ibid.*, Ins. no. 53 verses 9-10.
55. *Ibid.*, Ins. no. 114 verse 41.
56. *CII*. IV, Ins. no. 98 verse 25.
57. *Ibid.*, Ins. no. 51 verse 23.
58. *Ibid.*, Appdx. 3 verse 40.
59. *Ibid.*, Ins. no. 45 verse 59.
60. *Kāvyamīmāṁsā* (G.O.S), p. 55 line 5.
61. *CII*, IV, Ins. no. 120 line 4 ff.
62. *Śukranīti* (Cal. Ed.) II. 137-30.
63. *CII*, IV, Ins. no. 42.
64. *Ibid.*, Ins. no. 88.
65. *Ibid.*, Ins. no. 90 verses 14 ff.
66. *Ibid.*, Ins. no. 111-12. B. lines 2-3.
67. *CII*, IV, Ins. no. 67.
68. *Ibid.*, Ins. no. 84 verses 11.
69. *Ibid.* Ins. no. 51.
70. Kane, *History of Dharmshastra*, vol. III, p. 178.
71. *EI*, vol, I, p. 327, vs. 7.
72. *IA*, vol, XVIII, pp. 238-239.

73. *EI,* vol. I. p. 334, vs. 21-22.
74. *Ibid.,* p. 333, vs. 8-9.
75. *Ibid.,* p. 334, vs. 16-19.
76. *DHNI.,* vol. II, p. 701, fn.2.
77. *SGAI,* p. 145.
78. *Rādharmakāṇda,* p. 45.
79. *CII,* IV, Ins. no. 62 lines 1-5.
80. *Ibid.,* Ins. no. 88 verse 15-16.
81. *Ibid.,* Ins. no. 105 verse 13.
82. *Ibid.,* Ins. no. 105 v.14.
83. *Ibid.,* Ins. no. 105 verse 15 and 106 verse 19.
84. *CASIR.* vol. XIII. pp. 133-58.
85. *CII,* IV, Ins. no. 74 verse 5.
86. *Vikramāṅkadeva Carita,* canto XVIII.v.93.
87. *CII,* IV, Ins. no. 108 v.4.
88. *Ibid.,* Ins. no. 116, line 5; *EI.* IX., p. 169 n.1.
89. This classification and nomenclature, however, differed from the aurhority to authority – see Chakravarti, P.C. : *The Art of War in Ancient India,* p.113.
90. *Ibid.,* Ins. no. 46 verse 34.

# CHAPTER IX

# ALLIES *(MITRA)*

The territorial boundaries of the dynasties ruling over Central India during the early medieval period were contiguous. This often led to disputes and the rulers had to maintain diplomatic relations with the neighbours. In ancient India, since the time of Kauṭilya the relations between the two neighbouring states were considered to be those of hostility. This natural hostility between the two contiguous states was the basic principle on which the theory of *maṇḍala* was based with its six-fold policy of *ṣāḍguṇya* comprising *sandhi* (peace), *vigraha* (war), *yāna* (march for war), *āsana* (neutral in activity), *dvaidhībhāva* (a dubious attitude) and *saṁśraya* (protection of the rising power) and along with this the four well-known measures *viz. sāma, dāma, daṇḍa* and *bheda.* Reference the four well-known measures occurs in the Karanbel Stone Inscription of Kalachuri Jayasiṁha.[1] That these aspects of the six-fold policy, though not directly mentioned in the inscriptions were put into practice by the rulers, is justified by actual incidents in the history of the dynasties. Protection to rising power (*saṁśraya*) has been referred to often in the inscriptions of the Kalachuris and justified by concrete instances in their history. Thus, the Bilahari

Stone inscription of Kalachuri Lakṣmaṇarāja II[2] and the Banaras Plates of Karṇa[3] describe the help that Kokalla rendered to a number of his contemporaries. The former record says that after having conquered the whole of earth, Kokalla set-up two pillars of victory *viz.* the well-known Kṛṣṇarāja in the South and Bhojadeva in the North. The latter inscription states that Kokalla's hands gave freedom from fear to Bhoja, Vallabharāja, Śrī Harṣa, the lord of Citrakūṭa and to king Śaṅkaragaṇa. Again, Yuvarājadeva's expousing the cause of Vīrapāla, the king of Kuntala and sending an army to fight against a confederacy of kings, as referred to in the *Viddhaśālabhañjikā* of Rājaśekhara, is well-known. Further, Kalachuri rulers' help to the Rāṣṭrakūṭas who were their relatives are well-known. Instances of similar nature can be multiplied from the history of the Paramāras, the Candellas and other contemporary dynasties.

To preserve peace and consolidate their power and prestige, the rulers of the respective dynasties often followed the policy of matrimonial alliances with contemporary powerful dynasties of India. Thus, Kalachuri king Kokalla himself married a Candella princess named Naṭṭādevi and gave his daughter to Rāṣṭrakūṭa Kṛṣṇa II. Another of his daughter (or a daughter of his near relative) was married to Pala king Vigrahapāla. Similarly, Kalachuri Yuvarājadeva I, according to the Bilahari Stone Inscription[4] is said to have married the princesses of Lāṭa, Gauda, Karṇāṭa, Kaśmira and Kaliṅga. According to *Viddhaśālabhañjikā* of Rājaśekhara[5] probably this king also married the princesses of Magadha, Mālava, Pañcāla, Avanti, Jālandhara and Kerala. His chief queen Nohalā was from

Chāḷukya lineage. Further, several princesses were exchanged between the Kalachuris and the Rāṣṭrakūṭas which maintained their cordial relations for several centuries. Similar instances of matrimonial alliances occurring during reigns of Lakṣmaṇarāja II, Karṇa, Gayākarṇa and Kamalarāja (of Ratanpur branch) are available in our records. Such matrimonial alliances, sometimes, helped to heal the strained relations of the bitter enemies. An actual instance is in the case of Gayākarṇa whose marriage with Alhaṇadevī, the daughter of Guhila princess of Mevar in a way united the royal families of the Kalachuris and the Paramāras (who were bitter enemies of each other since the past several generations) and healed the sores of many generations.

Among the Paramāras, Udayāditya's daughter Śhyāmaladevī was married to Guhila king probably with the objective of bringing about peace. Prince Jagaddeva gave his daughter in marriage to Varman king of East Bengal. Arjunavarman's first queen was the daughter of a Kuntala king and second a Chāḷukya princess. The Gaṅga king Narasiṁha married the daughter of a king of Malwa. A Gujarat prince married the princess of Paramāra dynasty. Similar instances may be multiplied from the history of the Candellas.

War was often lauded in Ancient India as the primary occupation of the kings and the writers on the art of Government called upon to be ever ready for the same. The motives of warfare depended upon the circumstances.

**Motives of Warfare**

A study of the political history of the early medieval dynasties of Central India shows that the aims of wars and the causes which precipitated the conflagration of hostilities, were indeed many. These may conveniently be classified as under:

**Ambition to obtain supremacy in rank and title**

The privilege of obtaining the coveted titles of *Cakravartin* and *Vikramāditya* often attracted the the kings of the early medieval period of Central India as kings in ancient past, to wage wars. From the Khairha and Jabalpur Plates of Kalachuri Yaśaḥkarṇa, we come to know that Gāṅgeyadeva obtained the title of *Vikramāditya.*[6] In the records of his enemies, he is often called *Jitaviśva.*[7] The Gopalpur Stone Inscription of Vijayasiṁha states that Karṇa "who dispoiled (other kings) of their royal fortune (and) planted his foot on the heads of eminent kings", proclaimed the attainment of the undisputed position of the seventh *Cakravartin* of North India.[8] Having obtained this position he, for the first time in the history of the Kalachuris, assumed the two high sounding titles of *Trikaliṅgādhipati* (Lord of the three Kaliṅgas) and *Nijabhuj-Opārjit-āśvapati-gajapati-narapati-rāja-tray-ādhipatya* (he who by his arms has acquired overlordship over the three *rājas viz.* the lord of horses, the elephants and the lord of men), in addition to the titles of *Paramabhaṭṭāraka, Mahārājādhirāja* and *Parameśvara* used by his ancestors. These titles were used by the successors of Karṇa also, though without much significance.

The Paramāra rulers often assumed epithets which have both political and cultural significance. Vākpati II assumed the title of *Srī Vallabha, Pṛthvīvallabha* and *Amoghavarṣa* of the Rāṣṭrakūṭas because he considered himself to be the successors of the departed glory of the Rāṣṭrakūṭas. Similarly, Bhoja was called *Sarvabhauma Cakravartin* and this was of political significance. Because of his cultural accomplishments he was known by the titles *Tribhuvananārāyaṇa*, *Śiṣṭaśiromaṇi* and *Sarasvatikaṇṭhābharaṇa*. High sounding titles of political significance like *Kānyakubjādhipati, Triśatirājyādhipati, Aśvapati-Gajapati-Narapati-Trikaliṅgādhipati* etc. were used by the Candella rulers also.

**Territorial Expansion**

The policy of territorial expansion was the most important cause that was responsible for frequent wars in the history of the early medieval dynasties. Their policy to get permanent possession of territories on their frontiers led them to disastrous warfares. A good number of wars with the other contemporary powers of India were due to their desire of territorial expansion. The Banaras Plates of Kalachuri Karṇa of (K) E. 793 states specifically that *Prasiddhadhavala* acquired the country of Pali to provide an adequate field for the activities of the illustrious princes who would be born in the family.[9]

**Suppression of the Feudatories**

Wars were often waged by the kings to bring under control their feudatories who, at times, taking advantage of the weakening influence of the centre, tried to assert independence. From the history of the Ratanpur branch of the Kalachuris, we know that the early rulers of Ratanpur who owed allegiance to the Tripuri branch of the Kalachuris, tried to renounce the subjugation during the reign of Jājalladeva I and Ratnadeva II by making independent conquests and by striking gold coins in their names. This impertinence was not tolerated by the Cedi ruler Gayākarṇa who sent a powerful army which, however, was routed. Attempt in this direction was once again made during the regime of Jayasiṁha, another ruler of the later Kalachuris of Tripuri, who sent a large army against his contemporary ruler Jājalladeva II. This again was not a successful attempt. In the history of the Tripuri branch of the Kalachuris, we come across reference to the revolt of another feudatory *viz.* Salakṣaṇa. This revolt was, however, subdued by Malayasiṁha, another feudatory of Vijayasiṁha, in the battle of Karkareḍi. Many such instances may be quoted from the history of the Paramāras and the Candellas.

**Love of Fame and Prowess**

Frequent references in the inscriptions show that love of fame and display of prowess and glory on the part of the rulers often attracted them to wage wars. The Koni Stone Inscription of Pṛthvīdeva II (K)E. 900 states that Ratnadeva's "sole delight at all places and times, was in the festivity of battle; whether, he was followed by a host of armies or was alone."[10] Similarly, the Gopalpur Stone Inscription of Vijayasiṁha states that the king "whose sword, black as it is (in fighting) with his enemies, produces, oh wonder! white glory."[11] The Kumbhi Plates of the same king states that Gayākarṇa was eager to expand his glory in all the quarters.[12] Hence, the kings are often compared in bravery to the mythological heroes like Arjuna[13] and Paraśurāma.[14]

**Help to Relations and Allies**

From the history of the Kalachuris we come to know that they often helped the Rāṣṭrakūṭa rulers who were their relatives. Thus, Kokalla I rendered help to Rāṣṭrakūṭa Kṛṣṇa II who was his son-in-law. Another son of Kokalla I named Arjuna also probably helped Jagattuṅga, the successor of Kṛṣṇa II, with a large army probably during his war against the Gurjara Pratihāras. Once again, from the *Viddhaśālabhañjikā* of Rājaśekhara we come to know that Yuvarājadeva expoused the cause of Vīrapāla, the king of Kuntala who had been dethroned by his kinsmen. The army sent by Yuvarāja fought in favour of him on the bank of Payoṣṇī, defeated the confederacy of the kings and placed Vīrapāla on the throne of Kuntala. Similarly, the Paramāra ruler Sindhurāja helped the Nāga ruler of Bastar against the Kalachuris of Ratanpur, and married the daughter of the Nāga king.

**The Code of Warfare**

The authors of the *nīti* literature prescribed that of the three kinds of military conquests *viz. dharmavijaya, asuravijaya* and *lobhavijaya,* only the first was to be followed. The code of *dharmavijaya* prescribed among many things that the wounded and armless opponents were not to be slaughtered; quarter was to be given to enemy who had surrendered; prisoners of war were to be treated well and given medical facilities; weary and sleeping enemy was not to be slayed, women, children and often servants, camp-followers, insane and wounded were not to be attacked.[15] According to Manu, concealed, barbed or poisoned weapons were to be avoided in warfare.[16] The seizure or destruction of enemy's property was to be avoided as far as possible. According to *Agni Purāṇa* temples and their property and the property of the private individuals were on no account to be seized.[17]

That the people during the early medieval period were not unconscious of these codes of military honour, is evident from the enumeration of some of them by Rājaśekhara, the court-poet of the Kalachuri king Yuvarājadeva I in his *Bālarāmāyaṇa.* "A foe should be fought (with) fairly but not assailed with false accusations", says Rājaśekhara.[18] Further, he states that one should not "strike at those who are unarmed"[19], and should not throw arrow at women.[20] He says that one should have "regard to the rules which heroes are bound to observe".[21] In practice, however, as in case of most of the wars in ancient India, these rules seem to be only in books. There are several instances of excesses committed in course of wars which are recorded in the inscriptions of the Kalachuris.

The Goharwa Plates of Kalachuri Karṇa states that Lakṣmaṇadeva II "was adept in plundering the king of Lāṭa. The Ratanpur Stone Inscription of Jājalladeva I"[22] of (K) E. 866 states that ".... was burnt by him (*i.e.* Jājalladeva I), after slaying immense army; and by whom was captured and then released at his mother's words, the group of (his) ministers and wives etc."[23] The Gopālpur Stone Inscription of Vijayasiṁha refers to the destruction caused in anger of the places of the enemies.[24] The Bilhari Stone Inscription of Yuvarājadeva II states that he destroyed the abodes of his enemies[25], the valour of his armies caused unending oppression to his enemies[26] and that "no mass of dust could rise from the ground, inundated as it was with the streams of tears flowing from the eyes of the wives of (his) enemies who were again and again taken captive."[27] Rājaśekhara refers in his *Kāvyamīmāṁsā* to the destruction of enemies' gardens.[28] That all these references were not fancies of poetic imaginations can be gleansed from the examples of actual incidents in the history of the Kalachuris. In his expedition against the Magadha ruler Nārayāṇapāla, Karṇa's troops, according to Tibetan accounts, sacked some of the sacred Buddhist institutions and killed altogether five men out of whom four were ordained monks and one was an *upāsaka.* It was ultimately, through the mediation of Buddhist monk Atiśa *alias* Dīpaṅkara that peace was established by signing a treaty between Karṇa and Nārāyaṇapāla. Karṇa can again be cited for an instance of broken pledge committed by him. In his alliance with Bhīma of Gujarat to attack the dominion of the Paramāras of Malwa, after capture of Dhārā, capital of the Paramāras, Karṇa, according to Merutuṅga's *Prabandhacintāmaṇi,*[29] violated the previous agreement and annexed the whole of Malwa with his country. This enraged Bhīma who attacked the Cedi country and probably penetrated into it. According to *Dvayāśrayakāvya* of Hemacandra,[30] Karṇa, seeing tbe danger, made peace with him by presenting him horses, elephants and the golden *maṇḍapikā* of Bhoja which he had carried away.

In short, it may be said that instead of following the high ideals of the code of military honour which was rarely practised in the history of ancient Indian warfare, rulers of the early medieval dynasties of Central India, like their ancestors, followed the common-sense advise of Kauṭilya and later concurred by Śukra that if a state has immense superiority over its opponent it should follow the chivalrous code (*dharmayuddha*) otherwise, it should have recourse to all methods of warfare, whether fair or foul.[31] It may be noted that *Mānasollāsa*, a work of 12th century A.D. refers to several kinds of *kūṭayuddhas*. According to it, in *deśanāśaka* warfare, villages were burnt down, in *janaṅgachedaka* warfare, enemy subjects were mutiliated, in *gograha* warfare cattle was carried away, in *dhānyahara* warfare, corn was plundered, in *bandigṛha* warfare, treaders and wealthy men were imprisoned and in *sthānadaha* warfare, houses and palaces were burnt down.[32]

**Protection to the vanquished Army**

An important aspect of the ancient Indian statecraft was that a victor should acquisce in the continuance of established beliefs, laws and customs of the vanquished people and that instead of seeking extermination of the defeated, he should be content with their submission and defeat. The Bilhari Stone Inscription of Yuvarājadeva II states that Lakṣmaṇarāja obtained the effigy of *Kāliya* wrought with jewels and gold from the prince of Oḍra after defeating the lord of Kosala.[33] The same inscription again referes to the "presents offered by the prince who submitted to him.[34] The Koni Stone Inscription of Pṛthvīdeva II of (K)E. 900 states "how many princes did he not protect when they sought refuge on the battle field ?"[35] The Sahaspur Stone Inscription of Yaśorāja similarly states that he (Yaśorāja) was "Sibi in protecting even a wicked foe who comes back to him (for shelter)".[36] Following the policy of "uprooting and resplanting", some of these princes might have been reinstated on their throne on certain conditions. This was one of the major factors for the growth of feudalism under the Kalachuris.

Diplomatic relations with the neighbouring kings were maintained by means of agents, various types of which *viz. Dūta* (ambassador), *Parimitārtha* (diplomatic agent) and *Nisṛstārtha* are referred to in ancient India literature. Ambassadorial ties, as we understand now, had not, however, developed by then. Though no inscription of this period refers directly to ambassadorial ties, an interesting example is mentioned in the *Dvayāśrayakāvya* of Hemacandra which makes Bhīma's (of Gujarat) ambassador Dāmodara refer to several victories of Karṇa *viz.* those over the rulers of Daśārṇa and Kaliṅga and the kings of Bhadrabhāṭa, Yanti, Ganti, Hanti, Vanti and Manti.

## REFERENCES

1. *CII.*, IV, Appdx. 3 verse 26.
2. *Ibid.*, Ins. no. 45 line 8.
3. *Ibid.*, Ins. no. 48 lines 8-9.
4. *Ibid.*, Ins. no. 45 lines 10-11.
5. Act. IV,
6. *CII.*, IV, Ins. Nos. 56 verse 11 and 57 verse 11.
7. *EI.*, vol. I. p. 222.
8. *CII.*, IV, Appdx. 5 verse 14.
9. *Ibid.*, no. 48 line 13.
10. *Ibid.*, Ins. no. 90 verse 10,
11. *Ibid.*, Appdx. 5 verse 25.
12. *Ibid.*, Appdx. 4 verse 16.
13. *Ibid.*, Ins. no. 48 verse 15.
14. *Ibid.*, Ins. no. 56 verse 24; Appdx. 4 verse 21 etc.
15. *Mahābhārata: Śānti Parva* 45. 12; 96. 3; 100. 27-29.

16. *Manu,* VII, 90.
17. *Agni Purāṇa,* 226. 22-25.
18. *Bālarāmāyaṇa,* Act. II. sl.39.
19. *Ibid.*
20. *Ibid.,* Act. III. sl 4.
21. *Ibid.,* Act. II. sl. 54.
22. *CII,* IV., Ins. no. 50 verse 8.
23. *Ibid.,* Ins. no. 77 verse 22.
24. *Ibid.,* Appdx. 5 verse 13.
25. *Ibid.,* Ins. no. 45 verse 23.
26. *Ibid.,* verse 27.
27. *Ibid.,* no. 45 verse 25.
28. *Kāvyamīmāṁsā* (G.O.S.), p. 91 line 15.
29. *Prabandhacintāmaṇi* (ed. by Jinavijayamuni), p. 51.
30. *Dvayāśrayakāvya,* Canto IX. verse 57.
31. *Arthaśāstra,* BK. X, Ch. 3; *Śukra* I. 350.
32. *Mānasollasa* II. 1038-82.
33. *CII.,* IV. Ins. no. 45 verse 62.
34. *Ibid.,* verse 60.
35. *Ibid.,* Ins. no. 90 verse 13.
36. *Ibid.,* Ins. no. 115 line 3.

## CHAPTER X

# CONCLUSION

Central India comprising of Madhya Pradesh and Chhattisgarh was a playground of political forces during the early Medieval Period (*c.* 7th century A.D. to 13th century A.D.) on account of the rule of powerful dynasties like the Pratihāras, the Paramāras, the Kalachuris, the Candellas, the Kacchapaghāṭas, the Yajvapālas, the Nāgas etc. Each of these dynasties played a dominant role in shaping the political history, not only of the region over which they ruled, but northern, eastern, western and southern parts of India, where they often carried on raids and established their supremacy. Their conquests were carried as far as Bengal and Orissa in the east, Gujarat in the west, Kashmir in the north and Kerala and Karnataka in the south. All these achievements were possible on account of solid structure of political organisation which they had established in respective territories.

Their political thought and organisation was based on the age-old Indian tradition that the state is to be regarded as an organised whole. This Organic or Organistic theory of the State comprised (i) the component parts of the society constituting the four orders (*varṇa*) to work for the promotion of *Dharma* so that ultimately the individual merged into society. (ii) The State (*rājya*) or body politic consisting of seven limbs *viz. Svāmī* (the king), *Amātya* (the ministers and high officials of the state), *Janapada* or *Rāṣṭra* (territory), *Durga* (fort), *Kośa* (treasury), *Daṇḍa* or *Bala* (army) and *Mitra* (allies). This doctrine of *Saptāṅga* which is the epitome of Hindu Political thought, served as the guideline for structuring the entire administrative organisation of the dynasties ruling over Central India during the early medieval period. We have already discussed the details of each of these elements of the administrative machinery in the preceding chapters.

Never had Central India enjoyed a higher level of political and cultural prestige than it did under the ruling dynasties of the early medieval period, and the greatness that this period will always be remembered in the annals of Hindu civilization. It goes to the credit of the strong army of the Paramāras, the Kalachuris and the Candellas that Central India enjoyed peace and prosperity associated with enthusiastic pursuit of learning and literature and art even when many parts of northern India were bleeding under heels of its Muslims invaders. While the soldiers of Islam were carrying fire and sword against all the scattered principalities of northern India, Central India lived in peace and prosperity, undaunted by the new menace and holding out as the last stronghold of the ancient Hindu Civilization. This was all possible on account of solid administrative machinery which was worked out. These were the monarch, the ministers, high officials of the centre and the state, officials at the district and village level and the various guilds and pañchāyats closer to the people. Undoubtedly, there was no democratic government, but the subject enjoyed a substantial amount of self-government, as the local bodies had an effective voice in the management of their affairs. In short, it may be said that the government during the period typified the best that could be imagined and left behind themselves a great tradition.

# BIBLIOGRAPHY

## Original Works in Sanskrit, Prākṛit and Pāli


*Āchārāṅgasūtra*
*Agnipurāṇa*
*Aitareya Brāhmaṇa*
*Āmukhamālyada of Kṛṣṇadevarāya*
*Āpastambha Dharmasūtra*
*Atharvaveda*
*Bārhaspatya Arthaśāstra*
*Baudhāyana Dharmasūtra*
*Bṛhadāraṇyakopaniṣad*
*Chullavagga*
*Dighanikāya*
*Divyāvadana*
*Gautama Dharmasūtra*
*Jātakas*
*Kāmandakīya Nītisāra*
*Kāṭhaka Saṁhitā*
*Kathāsaritsāgara*
*Kauṭilya Arthaśāstra*, ed. Shamshastri
*Mahābhārata*
*Mālavikāgnimitra*
*Manusmṛti*
*Mārkaṇḍeya Purāṇa*
*Mṛcchakaṭika*

*Nāradasmṛti*
*Nītimayūkha by Nīlakaṇṭha*
*Pañcatantra*
*Pañcaviṁśa Brāhmaṇa*
*Pratijñāyaugandhanārāyaṇa by Bhāsa*
*Raghuvaṁśa*
*Rājanītiratnākara by Chandesvara*
*Rājanītiprakāśa by Mitramiśra*
*Rājataraṅginī*
*Rāmāyaṇa*
*Ṛgveda*
*Śatapatha Brāhmaṇa*
*Śukranīti*
*Taittirīya Brāhmaṇa*
*Taittirīya Saṁhitā*
*Vasiṣṭha Dharmasūtra*
*Viṣṇu Dharmasūtra*
*Yājñavalkyasmṛti*
*Yajurveda*

**Inscriptions**

Hiralal, R. B., *Inscriptions of C.P. and Berar*, Nagpur, 1932.
Mirashi, V.V., *Corpus Inscriptionum Indicarum*, vol. IV, pt. I-II, Ootacumund, 1955.
Delhi,198, 1987, 1991.
Ahmedabad, 1979.
Mittal, A.C., *Inscriptions of the Imperial Paramāras*,
Trivedi, H.V., *Ibid.*, vol. VII, pt. I,II,III, *Inscriptions of the Paramāras, Candellas and Kacchapaghātas*,

**Modern Works on Ancient Indian Polity**

Aiyangar, K.V.R., *Some Aspects of Ancient Indian Polity*, Madras, 1935.

Altekar, A.S., *History of the Village Communities in Western India*, Bombay, 1926.

Altekar, A.S., *State and Government in Ancient India*, Delhi, 2005 (rep. ed.).

Anjariya, J.J., *The Nature and Grounds of Political Obligations in The Hindu State*, London, 1935.

Banerji, P.N., *Public Administration in Ancient India*, London, 1916.

Basu, P.C., *Indo Aryan Polity*, Lucknow.

Bhandarkar, D.R., *Some Aspects of Ancient Indian Polity*, Varanasi, 1929.

Dikshitar, V.R.R., *Hindu Administrative Institutions*, Madras, 1929.

Dikshitar, V.R.R., *Mauryan Polity*, Madras, 1932.

Ghoshal, U.N., *A History of Indian Political Theories*, Calcutta, 1923.

Ghoshal, U.N., *Hindu Revenue System*, Calcutta, 1923.

Ghoshal, U.N., *History of Public Life in Ancient India*, vol. I, Calcutta, 1944.

Jayaswal, K.P., *Hindu Polity*, Calcutta, 1924.

Kane, P.V., *History of Dharmashstra*, vol III, ch. I-X.

Law, N.N., *Aspects of Ancient Indian Polity*, Oxford, 1921.

Law, N.N., *Inter-State Relations In Ancient India*, Calcutta, 1920.

Law, N.N., *Studies in Ancient Indian Polity*, London.

Mahalingam, T.V., *South India Polity*, Madras, 1955.

Majumdar, R.C. *Corporate Life in Ancient India*, Calcutta, 1922.

Mathai, J., *Village Government in British India*, London, 1915.
Mookerji, R.K., *Local Self Government in Ancient India*, Oxford, 1920.
Prasad, Beni, *The Political Theory in Ancient India*, Allahabad, 1927.
Prasad, Beni, *The State in Ancient India*, Allahabad, 1928.
Pratapgiri, R., *Problem of Indian Polity*, Bombay, 1935.
Sen, A.K., *Studies in Ancient Indian Political Thought*, Calcutta, 1926.
Sinha, H.N., *Sovereignty in Ancient Indian Polity*, London, 1938.
Vandopadhyay, N.C., *Development of Hindu Polity and Political Theories*, Calcutta, 1927.
Verma, V.P., *Studies in Hindu Political Thought and its Metaphysical Foundations*, Delhi, 1954.
Vishvanathan, *International Law in Ancient India*, London, 1925.

**Other Works**

Altekar, A.S., *The Rashtrakutas and their Times*, Poona, 1934.
Apte, *Rajasekhara, His Life and Writings.*
Beohar, R.S., *Tripuri Ka Itihas*, Jabalpur, 1939.
Bhatia, P., *The Paramaras*, Delhi, 1970.
Bhattacharya, P.K., *Historical Geography of Madhya Pradesh*, Delhi, 1977.
Bose, A.N., *Social and Rural Economy of Northern India.*
Bose, N.S., *History of the Candellas of Jejakabhukti*, Calcutta, 1956.
Chakravorty, P.C., *The Art of War in Ancient India*, Dacca, 1941.
Dikshit, R.K. *Candellas of Jejakabhukti*, Delhi, 1977.

Ganguly, D.C., *History of the Paramara Dynsaty*, Dacca, 1933.
Gupta, P.L., *Prachin Chhattisgarh*, Raipur, 1973.
Jain K.C., *Madhya Pradesh through the Ages*, vol. I, II, Delhi, 1977.
Majumdar, B.P., *Socio-Economic History of Northern India*, Calcutta, 1960.
Majumdar, A.K., *The Chalukyas of Gujarat*, Bombay, 1956.
Majumdar, R.C., (ed.), *The Classical Age.*
———————, The *Age of Imperial Kanauj.*
———————, *The Struggle for Empire.*
Mirashi, V.V., *Kalachuri Naresh aur Unka Kal*, Bhopal.
Mitra, S.K., *The Early Rulers of Khajuraho*, Clacutta, 1955.
Munshi, K.M., *The Glory that was Gujaradesha*, pt. III.
Niyogi, R., *The History of the Gahadavala Dynsaty*, Clacutta, 1959.
Puri, B.N., *The History of the Gurjara Pratihāras*, Bombay, 1957.
Ray, H.C., *Dynastic History of Northern India*, vol. I-II, Calcutta, 1936.
Reu, B.N., *Raja Bhoja*, Allahabad, 1932.
Sachau, *Alberuni's India*, London, 1910.
Shastri, A.M., *Tripuri*, Bhopal, 1971.
Sharma, R.K., *The Kalachuris and their Times*, Delhi, 1980.
Sharma, R.K., *Kalachuri Rajvansh aur Unka Yug*, vol. I, II, Delhi, 1988.
Shukla, Hiralal, *Prachin Bastar*, Nagpur, 1978.
Vaidya, C.V., *History of Medieval Hindu India*, Poona 1921-26.

**Journals and Gazetteers**

*Ancient India*, New Delhi.
*Annals of the Bhandarkar Oriental Research Institute*, Poona.

*Epigraphia Indica*, Ootacumund.

Gazetteers of the Different districts of Madhya Pradesh and Chhattisgarh.

*Indian Antiquary*, Bombay.

*Indian Culture*, Calcutta.

*Indian Historical Quarterly*, Calcutta.

*Jour. Asiatic Society of Bengal*, Calcutta.

*Jour. Bihar Orissa Research Society*, Patna.

*Jour. M.P. Itihasa Parishad*, Bhopal.

*Jour. Indian History*, Trivandrum.

*Jour. Numismatic Society of India*, Banaras.

*Jour. U.P. Historical Society*, Lucknow.

# INDEX